Amy Robsart

BY

VICTOR HUGO

Fredonia Books
Amsterdam, The Netherlands

Amy Robsart

by
Victor Hugo

ISBN: 1-58963-474-8

Copyright © 2001 by Fredonia Books

Fredonia Books
Amsterdam, The Netherlands
http://www.fredoniabooks.com

All rights reserved, including the right to reproduce this book, or portions thereof, in any form.

In order to make original editions of historical works available to scholars at an economical price, this facsimile of the original edition is reproduced from the best available copy and has been digitally enhanced to improve legibility, but the text remains unaltered to retain historical authenticity.

AMY ROBSART

DRAMATIS PERSONÆ

Dudley, Earl of Leicester.
Richard Varney.
Sir Hugh Robsart.
Flibbertigibbet.
Alasco.
Lord Sussex.
Lord Shrewsbury.
Foster.
Elizabeth, Queen of England.
Amy Robsart.
Janet.

Lords, Ladies, Guards, Pages.

Time. 1575.

AMY ROBSART.

ACT I.

SCENE.—*A large gothic chamber. Glass door at back, open window on right. A chair of state with double seat, surmounted by the coronets of an earl and countess; black velvet drapery conceals the legs of this chair. A table with twisted legs.*

SCENE I.

EARL OF LEICESTER, VARNEY. *Both enter speaking.*
LEICESTER *places a little iron box on the table.*

LEICESTER.

Thou 'rt right, Varney, though thy counsel be hardly that of my conscience. To avow my secret marriage with Amy Robsart to the Queen is at present impossible. Elizabeth does me the rare and distinguished honour of visiting me in my castle of Kenilworth. She will be here in some hours, bringing in her train my antagonist, or rather my enemy, the Earl of Sussex, to whom she would reconcile me.

VARNEY.

Now, the Virgin Queen, as people call her, does not willingly allow that those who aspire to her favour be, any more than herself, swayed by the human law of love. To confess, then, that neither your heart nor hand is free would be to give the Earl of Sussex such an advantage —

LEICESTER (*interrupting him impatiently*).

I tell thee, Richard, I shall do whatever thou wishest, whatever the difficulty of the situation demands; but for all that, my soul is not the less filled with trouble and anguish. What is royal favour in comparison with domestic happiness? What is the enmity of Elizabeth when pitted against Amy's love?

VARNEY.

If my lady had heard the Earl of Leicester draw that parallel, her heart would have been penetrated with gratitude.

LEICESTER.

My darling Amy!

VARNEY.

If my lord of Sussex had heard the Earl of Leicester heave that amorous sigh, his heart would have been swelled with hope.

LEICESTER.

Sussex! Sussex! I have resolved to keep silent, I tell thee! Yet if the Queen discover without me that which thou dost prevent me from discovering to her myself—

VARNEY.

Do not be alarmed, my lord. The ruins of the old mansion of Kenilworth are so placed as to escape the prying curiosity of everybody. It is at a distance from the new castle, and is believed to be both uninhabitable and uninhabited. And, in sooth, if the mysterious dove of my lord did not find a nest therein, one might say — even though it still harboured our surly old warder, Tony Foster — that the owls were its only tenants.

LEICESTER.

'T is well; leave me, Varney. Go, give an eye to the preparations for the reception of the Queen. I must speak to our worthy astrologer.

VARNEY (*affecting surprise*).

What! you have brought Alasco here, my lord?

LEICESTER.

Yes, on yesterday. Didst not know it? He is confined in the secret chamber, above. Have some provisions brought him, Varney, while I question him on a certain horoscope.

VARNEY.

Enough, my lord. [VARNEY *bows and withdraws.*

SCENE II.

LEICESTER *alone.*

LEICESTER (*slowly approaching one of the windows*).

Not a cloud in the sky. Ah, if it be true that our destiny can be subjected to the action of the stars that sparkle over our heads, never was the revelation of their influence more needed by me than at this very moment, for my earthly path is darkened and confused.

[*He sits near the table, opens the iron casket, and draws from it a small parchment inscribed with cabalistic signs.*

I cannot withdraw my eyes from these mysterious signs, traced by the hand of Alasco. Am I right, in good truth, in trusting to these lofty predictions? What would England say if it knew that at this hour the noble Earl of Leicester, the all-powerful favourite of Elizabeth, was seeking, like a child, to read his destiny in the symbolic lines of an astrologer? And yet, hath not my weakness been shared by all who have cherished some supreme ambition in their hearts? Vulgar destinies need no horoscope; but, before crossing the Rubicon, more than once did Cæsar take counsel with the prophetesses of the Gauls!

[*He approaches the wall at the back, opens a little concealed door, and, after looking round him anxiously, calls in a muffled voice.*

Alasco! Demetrius Alasco!

[*A little man, advanced in years, descends a narrow dark stair. He is clad in a grey, flowing robe. He is baldheaded, with white beard and grey eyebrows.*

SCENE III.

LEICESTER, ALASCO.

ALASCO.

At your service, my lord.

LEICESTER (*showing him the parchment*).

Dost thou know, old man, that in this thou hast given expression to many audacious fancies? This night no cloud has dimmed the sky, and so to thee it must have been an open book. The stars have not, then, confirmed these rash predictions of thine?

ALASCO.

I have, on the contrary, seen again, my son, in your star that which it has already revealed. Earl of Leicester, great is thy ambition, but greater still shall be thy fortune!

LEICESTER.

Then thou wouldst have really caught a glimpse of something through the shadow of my destiny?

ALASCO.

Need I repeat it? A throne. And what a throne! The first of the world!

LEICESTER.

Old man, dost weigh thy words?

ALASCO.

You ask the truth, my lord. I know it is not always prudent to tell it to those who are masters of the earth.
[*At this moment* LEICESTER *happens to catch the false and piercing eye of* ALASCO *fixed on him. He quickly places his hand on his dagger.*

LEICESTER.

Wretch! thou deceivest me! By the soul of my ancestors, thou dost dare to palter with me! Thou shalt pay dear for thy impudent jest.

ALASCO.

He jesteth not who hath his eye on heaven, his foot in the grave! Listen, my son. To-day it is full April moon in the great Chaldean arc. It has been announced to me that on this day your unworthy servant was to incur a mortal peril, from which he would escape safe and sound. I am old, feeble, and defenceless, and you are young, strong, and armed; yet I have more confidence than you in the double prognostications: your star has not lied, and you will not kill me.

LEICESTER.

The proof! the proof! Give me proof that I am not the dupe of an impostor!

ALASCO.

The proof? The proof is that while predicting a royal future I am not ignorant of the obstacles the past throws in its way.

LEICESTER.

How? What obstacles? What dost thou mean? Who has told thee?

ALASCO.

Remember, my son that you had me dragged yesterday like a wild beast from my obscure retreat; that a carriage closed to every eye conducted me to this donjon, isolated from all the abodes of men; that no human voice has struck my ear for twenty-four hours; and that, deprived of food and sleep, as the cabalistic law prescribes, I have spent the night in this narrow turret, studying for you, with my dim eyes, the book that has no leaves. Now question me, and try to discover if human agency could have taught me that this ruin is not deserted, as is believed, and that it conceals from the world an inmate —

LEICESTER.

God! Stop! silence! He is right. How could he have known?

ALASCO (*drawing a parchment from his bosom and appearing to examine it attentively*).

The irregularity of the stellar zones indicates that the birth of the young girl, although honourable, is inferior to the rank of the noble earl. Nevertheless, the crossing of the lines announces a legitimate marriage, which is kept secret, as the neighbourhood of the nebulous chormith proves. But this marriage cannot fail to be dissolved; for the pale star of the young lady will disappear in the hair of the great comet from the southern quarter, which draws in its train the beautiful star of the glorious Earl, and represents —

LEICESTER.

And represents? Finish! wretch, finish!

ALASCO.

Do you insist, my lord?

LEICESTER.

Make haste, I order you.

ALASCO.

I am but an impotent old man; that which my mouth utters, my mind has not conceived.

LEICESTER.

Speak, I say! wilt speak?

ALASCO.

The great crowned comet represents a high and sovereign dame who is to come from the south —

LEICESTER.

What is he saying? Old man, what dost thou hide under these mysterious words? Who is — who is, I say, this puissant personage?

ALASCO.

The Earl of Leicester is not ignorant of the symbols of heraldry; he will be able to recognize her by her crown.

LEICESTER.

Heavenly powers!

ALASCO.

This sovereign brings with her hither a vague tenderness — that shall become clearer and stronger. And perhaps — What is love compared to ambition? The hand that bestows a sceptre is not refused. The lord of this castle is not accustomed to halt on the road of greatness —

LEICESTER (*bewildered*).

Enough, old man, enough! You speak to me of the future, and your voice troubles my soul, as if 't were the voice of remorse!

ALASCO.

Good my lord, if —

LEICESTER.

Enough, I tell the! Alasco, if thou valuest thy life, bear this always in mind: he who knows everything must know how to be secret about everything. I will reward thy words generously, — thy silence more generously still. [*He throws him a purse of gold.*

[VARNEY *returns, followed by a servant carrying a basket containing refreshments. The servant places the basket on a piece of furniture and goes out.*

SCENE IV.

LEICESTER, ALASCO, VARNEY.

VARNEY.

Your orders are executed, my lord. The Castle of Kenilworth is ready to receive her Majesty the Queen.

LEICESTER.

I am now going to get myself ready, and shall return here immediately, to comply with a gracious wish expressed by the lady of the house. Do you, Varney, take care of Alasco. Pay him all the respect his age and learning demand. [VARNEY *bows*. LEICESTER *leaves*.

SCENE V.

ALASCO, VARNEY.

VARNEY (*regarding* ALASCO *with a smile*).

Well, thou old devil's cub, so our master, — thine and mine, — is thy dupe? The royal lion of England has been caught in thy snare, fox?

ALASCO.

You might express yourself in more seemly fashion, my son. If my science —

VARNEY (*interrupting*).

Thy science! Go to! Lay aside the mask with me who know thy face. Wilt dare tell me thou hast truly read in the stars the astounding revelations which thou hast just made to the Earl?

ALASCO.

At least, mysterious means —

VARNEY.

Yes, yes; a parchment a nimble and stealthy messenger of mine glided into thy hand yesterday evening on thy arrival.

ALASCO.

Ah! Then the young man who spoke to me in the darkness came from you? Who was he, prithee? His voice sounded familiar to me.

VARNEY.

A page the devil has placed at my disposal. So thou hast known how to profit by the information he brought thee.

ALASCO.

Why not? It left me a little precious time for the more useful purpose of observing occult nature for the conquest of the universal science. One step more and I shall have penetrated into the recesses of the laboratory of creation, shall hold in my hands the generating principle of gold! And then it will be my turn to be thy master, insolent favourite of the favourite!

VARNEY.

Tut! tut! Master Alasco, let us not quarrel! I have such faith in thy science that were I to lose thy favour I were fain to eat nothing but fresh eggs for the next three months.

ALASCO.

Thou saucy fellow! *my* philters! my draughts! Dost think I would waste them on thee? Dost think I would expend for sake of thy miserable life those sublime quintessences of rarest plants, of purest minerals, wherein are concentrated so many precious elements that the domains of a Leicester would not pay for a single phial of them. Rest easy, Varney! Though, in good sooth, one could extract more venom from thy body than from a viper, thou 'rt not worth a drop of my poisons.

VARNEY.

Nothing thou hast spoken so far has reassured me so much as thy last words.

ALASCO.

And as for penetrating thy master's secrets without thy aid, Richard Varney, I could do so as readily as I have penetrated thine!

VARNEY.

My secrets? It is not hard, by my faith, to know them. I have none.

ALASCO.

Of a truth? This clandestine marriage of Leicester, the breaking of which thou hast so much at heart, — it is his interest that moves thee solely, is it not? — because 't would stop him in his splendid career?

VARNEY.

Granted; and perhaps, too, to exchange the livery of a nobleman's equerry for the mantle of a king's master of the horse.

ALASCO.

And for this alone, my subtle Varney? Thou wert the screen under which the brilliant Earl of Leicester was introduced to the beautiful Amy Robsart; it was while taking shelter behind thee that, wishing to seduce Amy but seduced by her, he made her his wife. For old Sir Hugh Robsart, the man who stole away his daughter is not Dudley; it is Varney.

VARNEY.

These secrets, O perspicacious Alasco, thou hast learned from my mouth.

ALASCO.

Yes, but there are others I have read in thine eyes. Thou hast taken thy comedy seriously, good master of mine; thou lovest Amy Robsart, and that passionately.

VARNEY (*with a forced laugh*).

I! — oh, to be sure!

ALASCO (*with emphasis*).

Thou lovest Amy Robsart passionately! And if thou insistest on separating her from the Earl, it is in hope that one day she will belong to the master of the horse.

VARNEY.

Silence! Who could have told you this? Not the Countess; she is too proud!

ALASCO.

Thy uneasiness proves to me I was not mistaken. If the Earl learned in what manner his master of the horse abuses his confidence —

VARNEY.

If the Earl knew in what manner his astrologer plays upon his credulity — Come! come! Alasco, let us remain good friends! Trust me, it is the safest plan for both [*Drawing near him.*] Hearken. Your laboratory at Pelham blew up one fine morning as if 't were a volcano of hell. You know that in the domain of Cumnor we have one ten times finer, wherein you'll find furnaces and star-studded spheres, left by a former abbot, and there thou shalt melt and puff and multiply and amalgamate and vaporize and volatilize quite at thine ease until the Green Dragon become a golden goose —

ALASCO.

Good! And for entering on possession of the fine workshop, what is expected of me.

VARNEY.

To do as I say, and be silent as to what I do.

ALASCO.

Be it so. But, before all, answer me this: Are they going to keep me long a prisoner in this deserted turret? I do not fancy being alone in this fashion during the night with the screech owls and buzzards.

VARNEY.

What is that? The sorcerer frightened, like a child, by darkness and solitude? Thou 'rt not making any gold so far, Alasco, and so dost not dread robbers. As to demons, they will surely leave thee quiet, in this world at least.

ALASCO.

There is not only this world; there is the other! And this very night I saw —

VARNEY.

Prithee, what? Thy master, Satan, furnished with his horns twelve cubits long, and his tail, which makes as many coils on itself as the spiral staircase of St. Paul's belfry, London?

ALASCO.

Laugh not, Varney, and speak lower. Yes, this night, at midnight, I have seen a spectre.

VARNEY.

Dost take me for Leicester, Alasco?

ALASCO.

Speak low, I tell thee! Varney, once upon a time I had a disciple, a pupil —

VARNEY.

Ay, a confederate.

ALASCO.

Silence, I tell thee! He was a queer being, capricious and malign, with the spirit of a devil and the nimbleness of a sylph, — resembling a child rather than a man, a goblin rather than a child. He was called Flibberti-gibbet.

VARNEY.

In fact, a proper name for a goblin.

ALASCO.

He had a prying eye and a penetrating mind; he made himself master of certain secrets of mine —

VARNEY.

What an imprudent youth!

ALASCO.

I was obliged to separate from him. I quitted Pelham, leaving my laboratory, my alembics, and furnace at his disposal. But in a compartment of this furnace I had forgotten a little barrel of powder!

VARNEY.

Ingenious negligence!

ALASCO.

I learned two days afterward of the explosion of the laboratory. My poor pupil surely found his death in it.

VARNEY.

The poor pupil at least carried away thy secrets with him to the grave.

ALASCO.

Yes, but he is bringing them back again from it! Varney, it was he! It was his ghost that appeared to me this night under the ogive of the turret!

VARNEY.

Is it possible? And what said he to thee?

ALASCO.

Terrible things, — things that hell, death, and he alone could know. With a frightful laugh he cast in my face what he called his assassination. I half fainted with terror —

VARNEY.

And under what form did the shade of Flibbertigibbet present itself?

ALASCO.

Under that of a young demon, with skin the hue of fire. Phosphorescent sparks glowed at the tips of his black horns in the moonlight.

VARNEY (*aside*).

It must for sure have been my mad little merry-andrew.

ALASCO.

Well, Richard, what say you of this strange vision?

VARNEY.

Now, is n't it a dream rather than a vision?

ALASCO (*shaking his head*).

No, no, Varney! The infernal powers are meddling with our affairs. We must be on our guard!

VARNEY.

An additional reason why we should be united, my good father! Alasco, it does not rest with me to restore thee at once to liberty; but I can secretly urge Leicester to do so. Do thou help me, and I'll help thee. The Earl is about to return, and must not find us together. Keep faithfully the alliance between us, and I'll do the like. Agreed?

ALASCO (*they shake hands*).

Agreed!

VARNEY.

Enough, my dear Alasco; farewell! [*Aside.*] Devil take thee, thou poisoning quack-salver!

ALASCO.

Good-bye, then, my dear Varney. [*Aside.*] May lightning blast thee, damned villain!

[*Exit* VARNEY.

SCENE VI.

ALASCO *alone, then* FLIBBERTIGIBBET.

ALASCO.

That man has no conscience; he does not believe even in hell!

[*Suddenly a piercing voice calls from outside the hall.*

THE VOICE.

Doboobius!

ALASCO (*starting*).

God! who calls me by that name?

THE VOICE.

Dr. Doboobius!

ALASCO.

Heavens! it is the name under which I am outlawed! And the voice is that of Flibbertigibbet!

THE VOICE.

It is Flibbertigibbet himself.

ALASCO (*hiding his face in his hands*).

Oh, God! and in daylight now! Pardon! pardon!

THE VOICE.

Pardon? On one condition.

ALASCO.

What is it? Speak! What wouldst thou?
[FLIBBERTIGIBBET *jumps through the open casement and appears, wearing a fire-coloured costume.*

FLIBBERTIGIBBET (*pointing to the basket of provisions*).

What would I? A piece of bread and a cup of wine.

ALASCO (*raising his head in surprise*).

Strange language for a ghost!
[*He examines* FLIBBERTIGIBBET, *who has opened the basket and drawn from it a flagon and piece of bread, which he eats greedily.*
But art thou not dead?

FLIBBERTIGIBBET (*eating*).

Yes, faith! — of hunger and thirst.

ALASCO (*touching him*).

Why, he is really alive, my poor Flibbertigibbet!

FLIBBERTIGIBBET.

Not thy fault, good master mine, — eh? And I would not ask better than to make thee die of fear in turn. But 't is nearly eighteen hours since the ghost has eaten, and his youthful appetite brooks not further delay. Every one must live, — even phantoms.

ALASCO (*aside*).

Alive! I don't know if I would n't prefer him a spectre! [*Aloud.*] So thou hast escaped the explosion, then? By what miracle?

FLIBBERTIGIBBET.

There was no miracle about it; it was by address. I took good care to find out your mine, my gentle master; and though it blew up, it was when I was outside.

ALASCO.

I swear, my child —

FLIBBERTIGIBBET.

Oh, plague take your oaths! I know you. I know, moreover, your secrets; and that makes you fear me, while I have not the slightest reason to fear you.

ALASCO (*aside*).

Confound the little wretch! [*Aloud.*] My dear Flibbertigibbet, let us forget the past! I assure thee that no one rejoices more than I do at thy return to life. But answer my questions. How is it thou 'rt here?

FLIBBERTIGIBBET.

I am here seemingly to help on the dark designs of your accomplice Varney with regard to the mysterious lady who is living here in concealment. Varney! One more player in the game into which I am beginning to see clear.

ALASCO.

But, tell me, why this odd disguise?

FLIBBERTIGIBBET.

I gave up my trade of wizard, — it was becoming too risky, — and have taken to the stage. I am one of the troop that is to take part in the revels with which the Queen is to be welcomed by the Earl of Leicester. I play devils and goblins in the masques of Shakespeare and Marlowe, and wear the costume proper to my service to distinguish me from the gentlemen.

ALASCO (*aside*).

The ape! [*Aloud.*] How do you like your new trade?

FLIBBERTIGIBBET.

Hum! not too much! I am tired of always repeating the same phrases and making the same grimaces. By nature I am curious, and I like to be free. I would fain play a real part and mix in a real intrigue. I scent one here which, methinks, is dark enough and very interesting; and so I have not rejected the proposals of this Varney of yours, while resolved to take only such part therein as suits myself.

ALASCO.

Well, wilt thou come back to me, then?

FLIBBERTIGIBBET.

Why not? — but with the same reservations and precautions. Have no doubt of that.

ALASCO.

As you like. I would rather fancy on my own account, a little more knowledge as to the mysterious lady, as you call her, and as to my Lord of Leicester, too than Varney chooses to give me.

FLIBBERTIGIBBET.

Ay, to aid you with your horoscopes, I do not doubt.

ALASCO.

The Earl and the lady are coming here in a few moments. If you could —

FLIBBERTIGIBBET.

Hear what they tell each other, and then tell it again to you? Nothing could suit me better! I shall be delighted, on my own account, to listen to a dialogue between the falcon and the dove.

ALASCO (*looking round him*).

You must be concealed somewhere —

FLIBBERTIGIBBET.

Here is my lord's chair of state, looking as if 't were made expressly for the purpose!

ALASCO.

Good! Make haste, I hear some one coming.
[*He helps* FLIBBERTIGIBBET, *who crouches behind the chair.*
[*Aside.*] If he were only surprised there and hanged from the gutters of the castle! What a riddance!

FLIBBERTIGIBBET (*under the seat*).

They are coming. Go back, Dr. Doboobius.

ALASCO.

Call me not by that name!

FLIBBERTIGIBBET.

Good! the serpent has cast his skin and taken a new one. [ALASCO *returns to the turret.*]

SCENE VII.

Leicester *wrapped in a cloak;* Amy; Flibbertigibbet *concealed. The Countess enters leaning on the arm of the Earl.*

AMY.

How good you are, my lord, to have kept your promise and given way to my humour! How kind to show yourself to your poor recluse garbed as beseemeth the great prince you are. Permit me to unmantle you.

LEICESTER (*smiling*).

Thou art like other women, then, Amy? The jewels and feathers and silks are more to them than the man whom they adorn.

[*He affects to resist the Countess as she takes the mantle from him and shows him dressed in his courtier costume and wearing all his orders. He is clad entirely in white. Hose of white silk, doublet of white satin, white leather belt embroidered in silver, mantle of white velvet embroidered in silver and decorated with the star of the garter.*

AMY.

Amy has proved to you, dear Earl, that she cannot love thee better in this glorious garb than she did when you came, a stranger, heralded by the sound of your horn, into the woods of Devon, in a simple russet brown cloak.

LEICESTER.

Thou speakest the truth, my love.

AMY.

And now, my lord, sit thou there as a being for all men to worship.

[*She leads the Earl to the great chair. He sits down*

LEICESTER.

But do thou come and share my state with me.

AMY (*sitting on a footstool at the feet of the Earl*).
I stay here.

LEICESTER.

Thy place is at my side.

AMY.

Not so; at thy feet. Let me be, dear my lord; I am better here; I am well thus. [*Contemplating him.*] How splendid, how magnificent you are, so attired, my lord! What is this embroidered strap around your knee?

LEICESTER.

This embroidered strap, as thou callest it, is the English Garter, an ornament which kings are proud to wear. See, here is the star which belongs to it, and here the Diamond George, the jewel of the order. You have heard how King Edward and the Countess of Salisbury —

AMY (*smiling, and lowering her eyes*).

Oh, I know — I know how a lady's garter became the proudest badge of England's chivalry.

LEICESTER.

This most honourable order I had the good hap to receive at the same time with three most noble associates, — the Duke of Norfolk, the Marquis of Northampton, and the Earl of Rutland. But must not he who climbs a ladder begin at the first round?

AMY.

But this other fair collar, so richly wrought, and bearing some jewel like a sheep hung by the middle attached to it, — what does it signify?

LEICESTER.

It is the badge of a venerated order, once appertaining to the House of Burgundy, — the order of the Golden Fleece. It hath the highest privileges attached to it; for even the King of Spain himself, heir of the House of Burgundy, may not, unless by assistance and consent of the Grand Chapter of the order, sit in judgment upon a knight of the Order of the Golden Fleece.

AMY.

And to what country does this other brilliant collar belong?

LEICESTER.

It is the Order of Saint Andrew, revived by the last James of Scotland. It was bestowed on me when it was thought the young widow of France and Scotland, the hapless Mary Stuart, would not have refused to wed an English baron. But is it not better to be a free lord of England than share with a woman that dismal and rocky kingdom of the north?

AMY.

I think like my noble Leicester. As to myself, I should consider the hand of Dudley preferable to that of all the sovereigns of the earth.

LEICESTER (*aside*).

Alas!

AMY.

What aileth thee, my lord? Dost thou think the love of a queen could be more tender and ardent than that of thy Amy?

LEICESTER (*kissing her on the forehead*).

No! oh, no! And nothing shall tear thee from my arms, my wife! My darling wife!

AMY.

Thy wife, yes. It is as thy wife that the daughter of an obscure country gentleman rests her head on the breast of the most glorious lord in the realm, — on that breast which is loaded with the badges of the most illustrious orders of chivalry of Europe But when shall I be thy wife before all the world, as I am before God and thee?

LEICESTER.

Whenever it be possible, dear child [*He rises.*] But now thy desire hath been gratified, and in despite of my happiness near thee I must bid adieu.

AMY.

A moment, my dear lord, a moment yet! When I ask thee to proclaim me thy wife before all, thou dost not, I hope, accuse me of empty pride and vain-glory. And yet how proud I should be to be recognized as the avowed wife of England's noblest earl! But, Dudley, I think, above all, of my unhappy father. What is he saying at this very moment? What is he doing? What must have been his desolation on that day when he rose without receiving his child's accustomed kiss! My poor father! Did he believe, could he believe that I was seduced and carried off by this Varney, your equerry?

Ah, this idea is to me unbearable! He knows thee not, my Leicester; and even if he had not lowered his daughter to the rank of Varney, he could never conceive her raised to thine. My love, release me from my oath. Allow me, at last, to run to him, to undeceive him, to restore to an old man his darling daughter, and to restore her as the spouse of the glorious Earl of Leicester.

LEICESTER.

One day, yes, Amy, — one day this shall surely happen; and, believe me, thou canst not wish for that day more fondly than I. With what rapture could I retire to console thy father in his old age, and casting aside the toils and cares of ambition, spend my life at thy feet, — at the feet of the most adorable and adored woman in Europe! But alas! we must still wait and be content to hope.

AMY.

But why? Who hinders this union, for which you say you wish and which the laws of God and man alike command? Ah, did you but desire it even a little, nothing could bar your wish; for never could greater power have served juster claim.

LEICESTER.

It is easy for you to speak thus Amy. You do not understand the requirements of rank, the duties of power! And you make this request of yours on the very day when I was about to ask you to keep yourself more closely concealed than ever. Do you not know that it is to-day, almost immediately, I receive the Queen in this castle?

AMY.

The Queen? Well, what better opportunity of disclosing our marriage to her could you have?

LEICESTER.

What are you saying, my unfortunate child? Do you know what a capricious and ephemeral thing is royal favour? Such a disclosure would destroy us both. Trust to me, my darling Amy. A happier time will come; and if it does not come of itself, I will summon it. Meanwhile, spoil not our parting by desiring that which thine own interest forbids me to grant.

[*In rising to embrace* AMY, *he pushes the chair, which suddenly moves back and discovers* FLIBBERTIGIBBET.

LEICESTER (*perceiving* FLIBBERTIGIBBET).

What is this?

[*He tears himself from the arms of* AMY *and rushes on* FLIBBERTIGIBBET.

What is this rascal doing here?

FLIBBERTIGIBBET (*slowly raising his head*).

You see, my gracious lord. I was present incognito at the conversations of the fair Meriandre and the fair Indamara; like the jealous Odragonal, I was listening.

LEICESTER.

Indeed? Well, thy listening shall cost thee thine ears!

FLIBBERTIGIBBET.

It is likely.

LEICESTER.

What art thou?

FLIBBERTIGIBBET.

Whatever is your good pleasure. A living man or a corpse. A corpse if your dagger wills it so; if not, a living man, and one who liketh the end of a feast better than the beginning of a quarrel.

LEICESTER.

Thou malapert knave, playest thou with the halter of thy gibbet?

FLIBBERTIGIBBET.

Since I can't cut it.

LEICESTER (*violently agitated*).

'T is some emissary of Lord Sussex and my enemies. Go to! thy boldness shall receive such punishment as shall make thy fellows tremble.

FLIBBERTIGIBBET.

They are not numerous. My Lord Earl, three things you can do with me at your choice: hang me as thief to the topmost branch of the forest; nail me as spy to the great gate of the castle; send me as wizard to hell in flame —

LEICESTER.

This assurance is far from usual! Yet boots me much to know who has set him as a spy here. Listen, rascal. Thou hast well deserved all these punishments, — nay, worse still than these. Well, thou canst escape them and gain pardon by telling me of whom thou art the miserable instrument.

FLIBBERTIGIBBET.

To save my life? 'T would be cowardice!

LEICESTER.

I can do more than give thee thy life. Thou art doubtless paid for thy trade as spy; say how much, and if thou add by whom, thou shalt have tenfold what thou 'rt promised. Reveal this wretched intrigue —

FLIBBERTIGIBBET.

To make my fortune? 'T would be baseness!

LEICESTER.

What! threats and promises avail naught with thee? Force will have more success. Who hath prompted thee to hide thyself there? Answer! if not —

FLIBBERTIGIBBET.

I care as little for speaking or being silent as I do for the seven branches of the Marvellous Lamp; and if you had asked me in a different tone, likely I would have answered you as you wished, the man who has brought me to this bad pass being a vile intriguer whom it would like me well to see punished. Only, high and mighty lord, silence being the only superiority which I have over you, I do not see why I should renounce it.

LEICESTER.

Ah, this is too much! [*He draws his dagger.*] Traitor, thou shalt die!

FLIBBERTIGIBBET.

Good! The secret shall die with me.

AMY (*terrified, holding back the arm of the Earl*).

My lord! Dudley! What are you about to do? To end our sweet love parley with a murder!

LEICESTER (*with the dagger raised*).

Ay, so that it end not in a catastrophe more sinister still.

AMY.

Ah! pardon for this poor creature, good my lord!

FLIBBERTIGIBBET (*aside*).

She is adorable!

LEICESTER.

Amy, stay me not! This wretch is a spy.

AMY.

No, my lord! Look at that ridiculous costume. 'T is some mummer; or, at most, a madman.

FLIBBERTIGIBBET.

'T is so, noble lady, defend me! We are related to each other. I am mad as the moon and you are beautiful as the sun!

AMY (*smiling*).

You see well he is out of his senses! Come, my lord. Would you poniard this defenceless creature before your Amy's eyes? Mercy! Pardon! From your chivalry I demand the grace granted of old to the ladies in the tourney. Grant me this poor life. Come, come!

[*She takes the dagger from the hands of the Earl, who regards her with a smile, and makes but a weak resistance.*

Give me this villanous dagger, sir, and let it be banished from its place near a heart which is all mine.

[*She throws the dagger through the open window.*

FLIBBERTIGIBBET (*aside*).

Villanous dagger! Beshrew me! And it was a real Toledo poniard, damascened in gold!

LEICESTER.

You are a child, Amy! In sparing that life you perhaps expose yours and mine.

AMY (*quickly*).

Believe it not! An act of clemency cannot bring ill hap. Besides, how could the lot of the eagle depend on that of —

FLIBBERTIGIBBET.

The bat. Let me pick out the animal for myself.

AMY.

Come, my lord, let it not be said that you refused me everything to-day.

[LEICESTER *clasps her in his arms. She turns quickly to* FLIBBERTIGIBBET.

Thou hast thy pardon.

LEICESTER.

Yes, rascal, but not thy liberty. I must have thee in safe keeping until I know who thou art.

FLIBBERTIGIBBET.

You see already, fair lord, a devil; but a poor devil, and not a bad devil.

LEICESTER (*calling*).

Hola! Varney! Foster! Janet! Some one!

SCENE VIII.

The same. VARNEY; FOSTER, *doublet of velvet and yellow stockings. They run in tumultuously.*

VARNEY.

What does my lord require? [*On perceiving* FLIBBERTIGIBBET; *aside.*] Ah, my little treacherous masker! What meaneth this?

LEICESTER.

You do your service very negligently, Foster. Who has allowed this fellow to enter?

FLIBBERTIGIBBET.

Scold not that clod-pate, good my lord. After the fashion of devils in all ages, I have made my way here through the key-hole.

VARNEY (*aside*).

I breathe again. He has not sold me.

LEICESTER.

Put this masker in the castle prison.

FOSTER.

In the tower where are the dungeons; very well, my lord. Whence comest thou, then, thou red-haired devil?

FLIBBERTIGIBBET (*laughing and looking at the costume of the warder*).

From the fens,—where I learned the art of catching geese with their webbed feet and yellow stockings.

LEICESTER.

Let this prisoner be kept closely confined. Nobody must communicate with him, but let him want for nothing and suffer no harm. Go.

[VARNEY *and* FOSTER *try to seize* FLIBBERTIGIBBET. *He frees himself from them.*

FLIBBERTIGIBBET.

A moment, my masters. [*He kneels before* AMY.] You are so good that you do not need to be so beautiful as well. Madame, to you the mummer owes his life; he hopes to pay one day the debt.

[FOSTER *and* VARNEY *drag him out with them.*

AMY.

You see well that he is more mad than wicked.

LEICESTER.

Ah! I have some vague foreboding — The solitude of this dwelling is violated. It is the small black cloud, — forerunner of the tempest. Adieu, Amy. I leave thee with Janet.

AMY.

Shall I not see you again to-day, my lord?

LEICESTER.

The duties imposed on me by the presence of the Queen permit it not. But to-morrow, when thou hearest the great bell of the castle give warning that Elizabeth has retired to her apartments, I'll profit by the respite.

AMY.

She must be very happy, this queen! she has stronger hold on thee than thy wife.

[LEICESTER *sighs deeply, embraces her, leaves and again returns.*

LEICESTER.

Farewell! farewell! [*Exit.*]

SCENE IX.

Amy, Janet.

JANET.

Oh, my lady, if you knew!

AMY.

What?

JANET.

In the new part of the castle there are such crowds and uproar of men and horses. There are instruments playing, and such fine revels in preparation; but we shall not see them. They say the Queen is coming, and we shall not see her either.

AMY.

Ah, I know all this; but if I were free it is not the Queen it would pleasure me best to see.

JANET.

You knew, then, my lady? Perhaps you also know—

AMY.

What next?

JANET.

The name of the old man who, like yourself, appears to trouble himself very little about the revels, and confines himself to prowling around the castle.

AMY (*quickly*).

How! What old man?

JANET.

A tall, venerable old man with a white beard. I see him often walking on the heights that command this ruin. He sits down in the brushwood and hides his head in his hands, or raises it to the tower like a hunter on the lookout for a flying bird.

AMY.

And is it known who he is, whence he comes, or what he wants?

JANET.

No; Foster fears he is a spy of Lord Sussex, and has been thinking of some means to get rid of him.

AMY.

Janet, as thou valuest thy life, forbid him troubling this old man! Tell me, where could I see him?

JANET (*looking through the open window*).

My lady, come here! Look, look yonder! He is passing by the foot of the hill!

AMY.

God in heaven! it is my father!

ACT II.

SCENE. — *The great hall of the Kenilworth Castle.*

SCENE I.

ELIZABETH, LEICESTER.

ELIZABETH.

Yes, my lord, yes, my dear host, it must be! You and my Lord of Sussex must be reconciled this very day. Forget not that such is the pretext for our visit to Kenilworth. It is also the pretext for that private interview which I have been happy to grant you. So without further words, reconciliation —

LEICESTER (*bowing in assent*).

Your Majesty —

ELIZABETH.

Enough, I am satisfied. 'T is all I demand. Speak we now of other things. Do you know, my lord, that this domain of yours is in naught inferior to our domain of Windsor! And your reception of us is worthy of duke or peer, worthy even of a king.

LEICESTER (*aside*).

Of a king! [*Aloud and bowing profoundly.*] All that which your Majesty hath deigned to honour with an indulgent glance, belongs to your Majesty; and in laying it at your feet, my sovereign liege, I but do the honours of what is your own gift.

ELIZABETH.

It is to me you owe all that I admire in this castle, — all that I am almost tempted to envy?

LEICESTER.

What Leicester is tempted to envy the possession of here, my liege, is what he never can possess.

ELIZABETH.

How is this, my lord? Does not all here belong to you?

LEICESTER.

Does all here belong to me, my liege?

ELIZABETH (*smiling*).

My lord, there is some boldness in your respectful bearing; and at the very moment you bend your head so humbly, it seemeth to us you raise your thought very high.

LEICESTER.

Have I been so unfortunate as to offend your Majesty?

ELIZABETH.

I have not said so, Leicester. Only, when you hold in your grasp all that man can wish for, — titles, riches, honours, — and at the same time speak thus in a place where everything attests your power, I ask myself what can be the further aim of an ambition which all this cannot satisfy.

LEICESTER.

My ambition! How little your Majesty knows of the soul of Leicester. Take from your unworthy servant his castles, his earl's coronet, his peer's robe, despoil him of all your bounty hath bestowed on him, leave to Dudley — become once more the poor gentleman you found him — but his father's sword and the donjon of his ancestors, and his heart will preserve in exile and oblivion the same gratitude, the same love towards his Queen.

ELIZABETH (*aside*).

Love! [*Aloud*]. Well, yes, I see your emotion and am touched by it. Dudley, methinks I sometimes see a cloud of sadness on that brow which ought to be radiant only with joy. What aileth thee? Why do you not bare your soul to my eyes? Am I your enemy?

LEICESTER.

I have a secret, in good sooth, my gracious liege. Such goodness should embolden me, perhaps, to —

ELIZABETH (*gently*).

You do not finish, Leicester. Do you fear that your secret might be guessed —

LEICESTER.

I fear, madame —

ELIZABETH.

Go to! your secret might be guessed, and yet you have naught to fear withal —

LEICESTER.

Ah, your Majesty —

ELIZABETH.

That name by which you call me restores me to myself. Alas! I sometimes forget that I am queen, to remember that I am woman. If I were like others, free to consult my heart, then perhaps —

LEICESTER.

Madame —

ELIZABETH.

But no, — it cannot be! Elizabeth of England must be the wife and mother of her people alone.

LEICESTER.

I have at least lost none of the precious favour of my Queen?

ELIZABETH.

No, Leicester, no! Quite the contrary! We were speaking, I think, of your fair domain. Why, then, are you unwilling that I should visit yon ruined donjon, which has such an imposing effect when seen from a distance?

LEICESTER.

That ruin is deserted, your Grace, and hardly accessible.
[*The door opens at the back; appears an* USHER, *who halts at the threshold.*

ELIZABETH.

Who is this, pray? Who dares enter here without an order?

SCENE II.

ELIZABETH, LEICESTER, AN USHER.

USHER (*bowing profoundly*).

I obey the instructions of your Majesty. You bade me introduce, before the reception of the two noble earls, an old gentleman for whom my Lord of Sussex has demanded an audience of your Majesty.

ELIZABETH.

Ah! I remember; I promised, in truth, my Lord of Sussex to receive an old officer who has fought under my orders, and has some complaint or other to present.

LEICESTER (*smiling*).

A complaint! Against me, no doubt?

ELIZABETH.

Sussex would not dare. But I must receive this gentleman.

LEICESTER.

My liege, I withdraw.

ELIZABETH (*with a smile*).

Go! [*She gives him her hand to kiss.*

LEICESTER (*bows, and on going out, says to the* USHER).
Introduce the old man.

SCENE III.

ELIZABETH, *then* SIR HUGH ROBSART.

ELIZABETH (*alone*).

Why am I queen? The daughter of Henry VIII. the wife of Dudley, — that can never be! And yet he is so grand, so noble! his glance at once so tender and so proud! But to marry him would be to abdicate! What do I say? Is it not he who really reigns?
[*The door at the back opens.* SIR HUGH, *in deep mourning, throws himself at the feet of the Queen.*

SIR HUGH.

Justice, madame! justice!

ELIZABETH.

Rise, sir! You approach your Queen in very bold fashion.

SIR HUGH.

No, madame; I will remain at your feet until you have heard me. Your Majesty will not refuse the august and last succour that is left me. You will not repulse an old man, an old servant, who has shed his blood for you, — an outraged father, who comes to ask at the hands of the Virgin Queen the return of a daughter ravished from his arms.

ELIZABETH (*in a gentler tone*).

Your daughter has been taken from you, then? Rise, I say! Your daughter has been taken from you? And who would dare to do such a deed in this realm of England, which God and the saints protect? Your name?

SIR HUGH.

Hugh Robsart, of Templeton.

ELIZABETH.

Are you descended from that Roger Robsart who did such valiant service to our ancestor Henry VII. at the battle of Stoke?

SIR HUGH.

Yes, madame; and as Lord Sussex will tell you, I have fought faithfully for your Majesty myself.

ELIZABETH.

Speak, then, in all confidence; and believe that we are as true a lover of justice as you are loyal subject.

SIR HUGH.

I had but one child, a daughter, gracious madame; and an old father, who is near the tomb, may be pardoned for placing all his pride and joy in an only daughter. Well, madame, an infamous seducer came to me, in my retirement, as a friend. He spoke with the guile of the serpent, and my daughter has followed him.

ELIZABETH.

In truth, I pity you. We who are a crowned Queen do not know how any woman can let herself be ensnared by the wiles of a man. But it seemeth possible, since your tale has no other burthen. And what, Sir Knight, is the name of the ravisher?

SIR HUGH.

He is — Gracious madame, he is one who has puissant protection.

ELIZABETH.

Well, is his protection more puissant than ours?

SIR HUGH.

Pardon, my liege! I am little accustomed to the language of Courts, and know little of the value of words. This ravisher is the equerry of the Earl of Leicester!

ELIZABETH.

Of Leicester! The most blameless man in all England has a seducer in his household! The name of this miserable equerry?

SIR HUGH.

This coward who attacks the virtue of maidens and flies from the swords of men is called Richard Varney.

ELIZABETH.

Richard Varney? — good. And your daughter's name is Amy, is it not? What has he done with her?

SIR HUGH.

Alas! madame, she is here, — even here. I saw her at one of the windows of the ruined donjon at the end of the park.

ELIZABETH.

What? Lord Leicester told me that donjon was uninhabited. Are you sure of what you say? Have you tried to enter?

SIR HUGH.

The door has been kept closed against me. It is no doubt because this ruin is deemed deserted that the scoundrel Varney has concealed my unhappy Amy in it.

ELIZABETH.

Old man, you shall have justice. God's death! We are the born mother and protector of the maidens of England. A base equerry seduce the heiress of an honourable house! My Lord of Leicester will be exasperated when he hears of this abominable deed. We promise you, Sir Knight, our influence with him against this Varney whose credit with my lord you seem to fear.

[*She goes to a table and affixes her seal to a parchment.*

Take this safe conduct before which all doors open, and assure yourself whether your daughter is really concealed in this donjon. You have our leave to withdraw, for the Court is waiting to be introduced. [*She strikes a bell. An usher appears.*] Conduct this gentleman, and let the two lords enter with their attendants.

[SIR HUGH *leaves by a lateral door. The great folding-door at the back opens, and leaves free passage to the Court.*

SCENE IV.

ELIZABETH, LEICESTER, VARNEY, SUSSEX, SHREWSBURY. *Ladies, Bishops, Peers, and Officers of the Queen. Knights, Pages, and Guards of the attendants of the suites of the two Earls. The two lords enter at the*

*same time through the great folding-door at back.
They salute the Queen and arrange themselves with
their partisans, each on one side of the scene. The
Queen is seated in the middle.*

ELIZABETH.

My lords, what means this? We bring you hither to
be reconciled, and you show your antagonism in the
royal presence! Come, draw near each other and join
your hands, which must never be separated when the
needs of our service require them to be united.

[*The two Earls bow, but remain silent in their places.*
My Lord of Sussex, my Lord of Leicester, have ye
heard us? What signifies this unwillingness to move?
this silence? Will neither of you take the first step?

LEICESTER.

My liege — [*Aside.*] An uncouth soldier!

SUSSEX (*aside*).

A foppish upstart! [*Aloud.*] Your Majesty —

ELIZABETH.

Yes, so we are called; and because we are so called,
noble Earls, you shall obey us. [*To* LEICESTER.] Dudley, you are the youngest, and he is your guest. It is for
you to take the first step. [*To* SUSSEX.] My Lord of
Sussex, to please me you would fly to a battle, and you
retreat before a reconciliation!

SUSSEX (*without moving*).

Madame, I were well content my Lord of Leicester
should say in what I have wronged him, since there is
nothing I have said or done which I would not be willing to justify either on foot or horseback.

LEICESTER.

And for me, always under the good pleasure of my gracious sovereign, my hand shall be as ready to justify my deeds and words as that of any man that ever bore the name of Ratcliffe.

[*The two Earls look haughtily at one another.*

ELIZABETH.

Which of you, my Lords of Sussex and Leicester, wishes to taste the fare of our Tower of London? We are here the guest of one of you. But, by God's death! look ye to it that we make not one of you our guest before many hours. For the last time, let me see you obey and join hands in mutual love. [*In an imperious voice.*] My Lord of Sussex, I entreat — my Lord of Leicester, I command you.

[*The two Earls look at each other in stubborn silence, still hesitating, but at last advance and take each other's hand.*

LEICESTER (*bowing*).

My Lord of Sussex, it is with the purest joy — [*Aside.*] A traitor who has me spied in my own house!

SUSSEX (*bowing*).

My Lord of Leicester, I am delighted — [*Aside.*] A felon who surrounds himself with poisoners and cutthroats!

ELIZABETH.

Why, this is well! Banish your jealousies and resentments. Henceforth let my two most faithful servants be at the same time two sincere friends. My Lord of Leicester, we wish to distinguish the visit wherewith we honour you by some token of grace to such of your retinue as you yourself may choose for such promotion. Whom among your officers do you deem most worthy of the honour of knighthood?

SUSSEX (*aside to* SHREWSBURY).

You'll see she will not think of mine!

ELIZABETH.

By the way, Leicester, is there not among your equerries a man named Richard? Richard — What is his name?

VARNEY (*low and quickly to* LEICESTER).

It is no doubt of me the Queen wishes to speak, my lord.

LEICESTER.

If I might venture to help your Majesty's memory, is it Richard Varney?

ELIZABETH.

Precisely, my lord. What do you think of this Varney?

LEICESTER.

He is a faithful servant of his master, and a devoted subject of your Majesty. His merit and his zeal are such as place him truly above his condition, and if —

ELIZABETH.

Is he here?

VARNEY (*eagerly*).

Here I am at the feet of your Majesty.

ELIZABETH.

Well, my lord, I am glad to be able to undeceive you as to the real character of a knave and a traitor who sullies your noble house. This hypocrite, whom you praise in such good faith, is but a vile ravisher. Would you believe that he has dared to seduce and carry off the daughter of a worthy gentleman named Sir Hugh Robsart?

AMY ROBSART.

LEICESTER (*with a cry of terror*).

Great God, madame! [*Aside.*] Ah, the spy of Sussex!

ELIZABETH.

I share your indignation, and shall further increase it by informing you that this villain has had the audacity to conceal her in the very house where to-day you receive your Queen.

LEICESTER (*thunderstruck*).

Just Heaven! madame, do you suppose — [*Aside.*] I am lost!

SUSSEX (*aside to* SHREWSBURY).

What does this mean? Leicester has turned very pale!

ELIZABETH (*to* LEICESTER).

My lord, you seem disturbed!

LEICESTER.

I acknowledge in fact, madame, that —

VARNEY (*falling on his knees, crossing his hands, and bending his head*).

Madame —

ELIZABETH.

What hast thou to say for thyself? Dost thou avow thy crime? Hast thou carried off this girl? Is she concealed here? Answer, yes, or no.

VARNEY.

Yes.

LEICESTER.

Wretch —

[*He is about to throw himself on* VARNEY.

ELIZABETH.

My Lord of Leicester, if you permit it, we shall inform ourselves touching this matter without your help. We have not ended our examination of your officer. [*Aside.*] How deeply he is moved! [*Aloud to* VARNEY.] Did the Earl of Leicester, thy master, know of this intrigue? Tell me the truth, no matter how high the head it touches, and fear not. Thine is under our safe-guard.

VARNEY.

Your Majesty wishes the truth? The entire truth, before high Heaven, is that my lord was the cause of the whole matter.

LEICESTER (*aside*).

The traitor! [*Aloud.*] Thou villain, darest thou —

ELIZABETH (*with sparkling eyes*).

Silence, my lord. Speak on, Varney! Here no commands are heard but mine.

VARNEY.

And I, like all, obey you. Yet I would fain not speak of my master's concerns to other ears than yours.

LEICESTER (*aside*).

To betray me at thy ease, thou viper!

ELIZABETH.

The concerns of thy master?

VARNEY.

Yes, my gracious liege, if your Majesty permit me to be so bold, I shall ask you to grant me a moment's secret audience. I might give your Highness explanations that perhaps would satisfy you; but if they were

public, the honour of a respectable family might suffer.
These are delicate matters.

ELIZABETH.

We are content. But if thou tryest to palter with us,
by the soul of my royal father, the people of London
shall be witnesses to the building of thy gibbet. Leave
us alone, my lords, for a moment.

LEICESTER (*aside*).

I am lost!

[*All withdraw save* VARNEY.

SCENE V.

ELIZABETH, VARNEY; *an Usher at the door at the back.
The Queen is seated;* VARNEY *remains on his knees.*

ELIZABETH.

Rise and speak. What hast thou to say in thy defence?

VARNEY.

I acknowledge, your Grace, that my crime would be
great if I had, as my dread sovereign imagines, taking
advantage of the weakness of a young girl, seduced and
dishonoured her.

ELIZABETH.

What is this? Richard Varney, have I been misinformed? Is the guilty man another than thou?

VARNEY.

No, the Queen has been correctly informed, but, gracious lady, you have not been informed of everything.
Mistress Robsart is not dishonoured, unless it be dis-

honour to be the wedded wife of the equerry of my Lord of Leicester.

ELIZABETH.

What? You have married her? Amy Robsart is then your lawful wife?

VARNEY.

My lawful wife, an't please your Majesty.

ELIZABETH.

Take heed thou deceive us not, sirrah! If thou hast married her, why accuse the noble Earl? What dost thou charge him with? May he not have been entirely ignorant of the matter?

VARNEY.

My Lord of Leicester was, in good sooth, entirely ignorant of the matter, yet is he, I repeat it, the cause of everything. Your Majesty may judge for yourself.

ELIZABETH.

Go on, we are listening.

VARNEY.

My noble master, that glory of England's Court, hath long since renounced marriage. Some secret anxious feeling, the cause whereof none can fathom, has made him fly from all of womankind. It is said my unhappy master — But, madame, am I to repeat what is said?

ELIZABETH.

Speak on! speak on!

VARNEY.

'T is said, my lord doth hide in the depths of his soul a passionate love for one so high above him that 't is not permitted him to hope.

ELIZABETH.

What? Still, methinks, there is no woman too highly placed to be out of reach of the noble Earl.

VARNEY.

Alas! your Highness must know well that there is one.

ELIZABETH.

What sayest thou? What dost thou mean? I do not understand thee, Varney.

VARNEY.

Guesses here are rash. Yet often have I seen my noble master, unconscious that he was observed, kiss a lock of hair. I had need to raise mine eyes very high to see its fellow.

ELIZABETH.

Well, well. You were saying then that your master—

VARNEY.

My lord, entirely absorbed in this passion, will not hear of marriage, either for himself or for any of his household.

ELIZABETH.

Poor, noble Earl!

VARNEY.

And so, being desperately in love with Mistress Amy Robsart, I thought I must conceal our marriage to 'scape dismissal from my lord's service. Have I not some cause to say then, gracious madame, that my master is the cause of this mystery and seeming crime,— that the fault is his?

ELIZABETH.

The fault is not so grave!

VARNEY.

I did but wait a favourable occasion for making a full confession to him; and now if your Majesty deign to say a few words on my behalf, I doubt not he will grant me pardon, at the same time maintaining me in my office and leaving me my wife.

ELIZABETH.

Yes, since Amy Robsart is thy wife I promise, Varney, to appease the wrath of thy master.

VARNEY.

Madame, my gratitude —

ELIZABETH.

And we are about to take such measure ourselves that Sir Hugh Robsart shall not blush for his son-in-law.

VARNEY (*bowing profoundly*).

The kindness of your Majesty doth penetrate —

ELIZABETH.

Enough, Varney; I am content with thy explanation. Usher! let the doors be thrown open.

SCENE VI.

ELIZABETH, VARNEY, LEICESTER, SUSSEX, *the entire Court*

ELIZABETH (*after a moment's silence*).

Your sword, my Lord of Leicester.

LEICESTER (*aside*).

The sword first, and the head after.

SUSSEX (*aside to* SHREWSBURY).

Would this mean his disgrace, I wonder?

[LEICESTER *unbuckles his sword and presents it to the Queen on bended knee.*

ELIZABETH.

Richard Varney, come forth and kneel down.

[VARNEY *obeys. She draws the sword from the scabbard; movement of surprise in the assembly, emotion among the ladies.*

LEICESTER (*aside*).

What is her intention?

ELIZABETH (*gazing on the sword with satisfaction*).

Had I been a man, methinks none of my ancestors would have loved the flashing of a good sword better. As it is, it liketh me to look on one. If Heaven had made me beautiful, it is in such a steel mirror as this I would fain arrange my woman's gear. Richard Varney, in the name of God and Saint George we dub thee knight!

[*She gives him the accolade with the flat of the sword.*

Be Faithful, Brave, and Fortunate! Arise, Sir Richard Varney. [*General astonishment.*]

LEICESTER.

Ah, she rewards the treachery of Varney before punishing mine!

ELIZABETH.

The buckling of the spurs, and what other rites remain, may be finished to-morrow in the chapel. Varney, your fortune has now had a beginning, but learn to temper your desires. I think it is that mad, gamesome fellow, Shakespeare, who says this: "Ambition doth o'erleap itself and falls o' the other side." Go!

[VARNEY *makes a profound salutation. The Queen turns to* LEICESTER.

Gramercy, my Lord of Leicester, banish the shadows from that gloomy brow of thine. The evil that was done has been repaired.

LEICESTER (*aside*).

What could he have said? [*Aloud.*] I do not yet know—

ELIZABETH.

Yes, my lord, you have been misunderstood; but the honour of your noble house has not been tarnished.

LEICESTER.

I do not comprehend, madame.

ELIZABETH.

You shall in a moment. But permit me first to ask you to do me a favour.

LEICESTER.

It is already done, madame, when you deign to ask it.

ELIZABETH.

It is to pardon your equerry Varney, — who, without your consent, has married Amy Robsart.

LEICESTER.

He! Amy Robsart! [*Shaking his clenched hand at* VARNEY.] Wretch!

ELIZABETH.

My lord, restrain your indignation. Since he has been so mad as to fall in love with her, and so culpable as to carry her off, you can hardly blame him for making her his lawful wife.

LEICESTER.

Thou shameless villain! hast thou dared —

VARNEY (*bending his head*).

Good my lord and master, it was the only means of repairing a great misfortune, — of saving what else was lost.

LEICESTER.

I cannot contain myself. This audacity of thine shall cost thee dear.

ELIZABETH.

My lord, you have promised us to pardon him.

LEICESTER.

Madame, it is such an affront!

ELIZABETH.

Not by any means such an affront as Sir Hugh Robsart suffered withal.

LEICESTER.

No, madame, I am going to tell you all. Alas! you do not know —

VARNEY (*hurriedly*).

Her Majesty knows all, my lord. She is acquainted with your invincible dislike to marriage, — a dislike so extreme that you cannot brook it even in the case of your servants. She knows that your soul hides a mysterious passion —

ELIZABETH (*quickly*).

Silence, Varney!

[*Drawing near* LEICESTER, *in a faint voice.*]

My lord, do you deny that secret passion he has the boldness to imagine? [LEICESTER *tries to speak.*] Hush! I understand and pity you; but be prudent, my dear Dudley!

LEICESTER (*bowing*).
Madame, such goodness! [*Aside.*] O torture!

ELIZABETH.
My lord, we will let Varney himself complete his justification to yourself. Sir Richard Varney, it is our good pleasure that your wife be present at our reception to-day.

LEICESTER (*aside*).
God!

VARNEY.
Your Majesty shall be obeyed. Such a favour does great honour to my wife and me.

LEICESTER (*aside*).
Insolent knave!

SUSSEX (*whispering to* SHREWSBURY).
He is now in greater favour than ever!

ELIZABETH.
Come, my Lord of Sussex, come, my lords and gentlemen, it is time to take your parts in the sports and interludes which the courtesy of my Lord of Leicester hath prepared for our entertainment.

SCENE VII.

LEICESTER, VARNEY.

LEICESTER (*with indignation*).
What hast thou done, thou false knave? My Amy to pass in the eyes of the world for thy wife!

VARNEY.

In good truth, my lord, I am guilty, — guilty of an insane devotion to your person. For whom have I adventured that reckless declaration? Who was on the brink of ruin? Who required to be saved? Was it I, poor and obscure, with nothing to lose and nothing to gain?

LEICESTER.

Go to with thine intentions! Was it needful thou shouldst say she was thy wife?

VARNEY.

Ought I then to let it be believed she was my mistress?

LEICESTER.

No, of a surety, no! but you ought to have — you ought to have —

VARNEY.

What, my lord?

LEICESTER.

Exposed me to danger rather than to shame. 'T would be better to have acknowledged everything.

VARNEY.

That was not the meaning of your furious look when you thought I meant to denounce you. Acknowledge everything! Overturn with a word the highest destiny in Europe, reduce to the condition of a simple country squire that illustrious Earl of Leicester who bestows peerages, appoints generals, distributes bishopricks, convokes and dissolves parliaments, the young and glorious minister for whom the very ballads of the people prophesy the most august of all unions! Excuse me, my lord, I freely grant that I had not such courage — or such baseness!

LEICESTER.

And yet, after all, is not all this greatness purchased too dear at the price of happiness? Instead of wasting my life in the struggles and perils of power, should I not be doing better, — ay, a hundred times better, — by living, as you say, like a peaceful country squire at the feet of my beloved wife?

VARNEY.

Peaceful? Pardon me, my lord, but I did not say peaceful. Beware! my lord. During the time I was speaking to the Queen, when the suspicion occurred to her that one greater than I might have been the seducer of the young girl, I saw gather on her brow all the jealous anger of the woman who loves —

LEICESTER.

What is this thou sayest? She loves me, you think, Richard?

VARNEY.

Ay, ay, she loves you! Her love for you has reached that point where rank is nothing, self-sacrifice a trifle, and every obstacle worthy only of laughter. We have seen a will less strong than hers break bonds less fragile than yours!

LEICESTER.

She loves me! Art really sure she loves me?

VARNEY.

I have only seen her vexation, but you have seen her joy. And now go to the daughter of Henry VIII. who loves you, and believes herself loved in turn; tell her of your marriage with a country damsel at the very moment she is perhaps thinking of offering you her royal hand; reveal to this Queen, who purposes making you a king, that there is already a Countess of Leicester; go, my lord, tell Elizabeth Tudor that she has a rival, go — and I say to you that you will endanger your own head, and a head that is dearer to you than your own.

LEICESTER.

Amy! my Amy in peril! Enough, Varney! What thou hast done has been done well.

VARNEY (*aside*).

Ha! I have him at last!

LEICESTER.

We must save Amy, Varney. She must perhaps pass — for being that which you told the Queen.

VARNEY.

Still, you must remember the consent of my lady is essential.

LEICESTER.

What sayest thou? Prithee, why?

VARNEY.

You have heard the Queen, my lord. She desires that my pretended wife be presented to her to-day.

LEICESTER.

It is true. God! O God!

VARNEY.

Do you think my lady can conquer her repugnance so far as to bear my name for a little time? She is the daughter of Sir Hugh Robsart, but I am now Sir Richard Varney.

LEICESTER.

It does not matter. She is Countess of Leicester, and as proud in her virtue as is Elizabeth of England in her power!

VARNEY.

Then let us not speak of it further. There is nothing to be done.

LEICESTER.

But we are lost, then! Varney, she is lost! Do not forsake me! Advise and direct me.

VARNEY.

How can I, my lord? Is it I who have influence and authority over my lady? Have I the power of convincing or the right of commanding her?

LEICESTER.

She loves me too well to allow herself to be persuaded to such a course, and I love her too well to speak as a master.

VARNEY (*folding his arms*).

Well, let us await the consequences of the fury of the Queen.

LEICESTER.

No, no. I must save her at any price. Hearken, Varney. Spare me a harrowing and most embarrassing scene with Amy. Speak to her in my name.

VARNEY.

Useless. She would not believe me.

LEICESTER.

You can at least try.

VARNEY.

'T would be a waste of time when we have no time to lose!

LEICESTER.

What if I gave you my orders to her in writing?

VARNEY

They should be decisive and imperious. You must give me full powers.

LEICESTER (*hesitating for the last time*).

Well, be it as you wish.

[*He goes to the table, writes a few words, and hands the paper to* VARNEY.

Is that sufficient?

VARNEY (*after reading*).

Yes, my lord. We must, however, take our precautions in case my lady, notwithstanding this written order, should refuse to present herself to the Queen.

LEICESTER.

What could we do then?

VARNEY.

The only thing in our power would be to conduct the Countess to your domain of Cumnor, by force if need be, and tell the Queen she has fallen dangerously ill. [*Aside.*] It is a domain in which Alasco rules.

LEICESTER.

What? violence!

VARNEY.

For sake of her own safety.

USHER (*entering*).

Her Majesty commands the attendance of my Lord of Leicester

[*On a sign from* LEICESTER *the* USHER *leaves.*

LEICESTER.

Well, well! I trust her, as I trust myself, to thy fidelity, Varney. And now I go to meet the Queen. Oh, what a situation is mine, — placed between two women, one of whom has the power, the other the right! [*He retires.*

VARNEY.

Yes, my master; and what renders the situation still graver is that you are at once weak and ambitious! [*Reading the paper again.*] "Amy, trust all that Richard Varney tells you. Whatever he does, it is by my order and by my will." Ah, now, proud Amy, you are mine!

ACT III.

SCENE. — *Same as in first act.*

SCENE I.

VARNEY, ALASCO.

VARNEY.

We are nearing the end of our ambitions, Alasco; one more effort and we shall have a king for our master. You say you think Flibbertigibbet might be useful to us? In good truth, he did not betray me yesterday.

ALASCO.

Yes, if you require for your expedition some one who is young, alert, and intelligent —

VARNEY.

Oh! my object is simply to get hold of a person who might be troublesome, and bring that person secretly to Cumnor. But who will answer for your pupil?

ALASCO.

He is at this moment, as the saying is, at death's door, and will be glad to get out of his unpleasant plight at any price. Yet such is the craft of the fellow that it would not surprise me if he were out of prison at the very time we are speaking.

VARNEY.

Tush, tush! he is not as cunning as this prison is strong. It has only one outlet, and this outlet opens on the passage between the dungeons. So that if I wished to rid me of thy pupil, I would open the door instead of shutting it, being careful first to draw the bolt of the trap-door, and would send him very quickly to frighten the rats in the cellars of the donjon by a visit made in the perpendicular.

ALASCO.

All very well. But how can you reach him. The Earl, in your presence, forbade Foster any communication between him and any one whatever, and his prison has, as you say, but one door.

VARNEY.

Yes, one visible door. But listen; there is another concealed one that communicates by a secret passage with the turret which you use as a laboratory. I alone know all the windings of this castle.

ALASCO.

As Beelzebub knows all the windings of thy soul.

VARNEY.

Not unlikely. Here is the key of the secret door of which I spoke. Find Flibbertigibbet, lay before him our proposal. If he accepts it, enlist the imp in our service; if he refuse, why, thou canst avail thyself of this visit to drop something in his drinking water —

ALASCO.

Good, good! Is that all?

VARNEY.

Not yet; I have kept the most important matter for the end. Thou must prepare, on the instant, a sleeping potion, which, administered in a given case, to a woman for example, may send her into a sleep at once, and that sleep so profound that she shall let herself be taken to a carriage, and may travel a whole night without awaking and, consequently, without giving the alarm or making resistance.

ALASCO.

I agree. And for whom is this potion intended?

VARNEY.

Ask the planets.

ALASCO.

Must I stop at sleep?

VARNEY.

Thou damned old poisoner, I order a harmless drink of thee, — harmless, dost thou understand? Harmless! dost understand the meaning of the word?

ALASCO.

Very well; I am not to be asked, then, to affect the House of Life?

VARNEY.

Take thou good care not to affect this house if thou'dst save thine own hovel! If thy dose be not as inoffensive as a glass of water, I swear to thee on my soul, thou shalt suffer as many deaths as there are hairs on thy head. Dost laugh, thou old satyr!

ALASCO.

Doubtless. [*Taking off his cap.*] I am bald, and then too, you swear by your soul.

VARNEY.

I hear some one walking in the gallery. Come, set about thy sleeping mixture; and mind, above all, it be harmless, thou devil's apothecary! I shall return to show thee the secret passage.

[*He pushes him to the secret stair, enters after him and shuts the door.*

SCENE II.

AMY, *a casket in her hand;* JANET, *with a mantle which she throws over the back of a chair; afterward,* FOSTER.

AMY.

Janet, open the window on the side next the new castle. Methinks I shall so hear better the tolling of the great bell which is to announce to me the near arrival of my lord. Make an end of my attiring. Quick, my necklace, my bracelets.

[JANET *draws them from the casket and fastens them on her mistress.*

JANET.

They are very white, these pearls; but this arm is still whiter. All the same, they are magnificent! I am sure every one of them must be worth —

AMY.

Fie, fie, Janet! All the galleons of Portugal could not pay for them; 't was he who gave them to me!

JANET.

You are very beautiful, my lady!

AMY.

May he think as thou dost, child! Alas! If I ever had any beauty, it has had to stand many a severe ordeal. My poor eyes have shed many tears since I left my father. My father! When I think that he is here, that he is near me! Ah, I am both afraid and anxious to see him. [*Enter* FOSTER.] What is your business with me, good Foster?

FOSTER.

My lady, you are about to receive a visit.

AMY.

A visitor to me, Foster? You forget your instructions; I am forbid to leave the castle, and no one is allowed to enter here.

FOSTER.

Yes, my lady; but when a visitor presents such a pass as this —   [*He hands a parchment to* AMY.

AMY (*casting a glance on the parchment*).

A pass from the Queen! Foster, let him enter. There is no door in England which must not open before this. [FOSTER *throws open the door. Enters* SIR HUGH ROBSART.

SCENE III.

The same; SIR HUGH ROBSART. SIR HUGH *stops on the threshold.* AMY *utters a cry.*

AMY.

O God! my father!
    [*She makes a sign, and* FOSTER *and* JANET *go out.*

SIR HUGH.

Yes, God and your father. Your father who is here in your presence, and God who has led him hither.
    [AMY *rises and runs up to him. He draws back*

AMY (*stopping*).

Father!

SIR HUGH.

Madame! I do not know if it is by that title I am to address you.

AMY.

Ah, these are hard words! Call me your daughter. You are my father always.

SIR HUGH.

Your judge, Amy.

AMY.

Oh, do not freeze me with that gaze! If you only knew—

SIR HUGH.

What? Finish! I will not condemn you unheard.

AMY.

And I have taken an oath. I cannot speak.

SIR HUGH.

Alas! do I not already know a part of the truth? Have you not left your father to follow your seducer, this equerry of Lord Leicester, this—

AMY.

Father, you are mistaken. Appearances—

SIR HUGH.

Appearances! See, I am in mourning, you in holiday garb. Is this appearances? Come, tell me, of whom are you the mistress?

AMY (*raising her head*).

Father, I am married!

SIR HUGH.

Married? Married to whom?

AMY.

To whom? Ah! that name must not leave my lips. I have promised — nay, sworn —

SIR HUGH.

I have my doubts about a husband whose name his wife cannot pronounce before her father.

AMY.

Once you would have believed my lightest word —

SIR HUGH.

Yes, once.

[*The tolling of the great bell is heard.*

AMY.

Ah, the great bell! At last! He is coming!

SIR HUGH.

Who is coming?

AMY.

My husband, father. Hearken, I cannot name him to you, but you can see him. Do you know by sight any of the lords of Elizabeth's Court?

SIR HUGH.

I have frequented camps more than Courts. Still, I know a few of them, — the Earl of Sussex, the Duke of Rutland, Lord Shrewsbury —

AMY.

Are these all?

SIR HUGH.

This morning I saw the young Marquis of Northampton — and (I was forgetting) the owner of this Castle of Kenilworth, the favourite minister of the Queen, the master of your seducer, Lord Leicester.

AMY (*leading* SIR HUGH *to the glass door of the gallery at the back of the hall*).

Come, my father, retire into that gallery; he whom you will see enter, in a few moments, is the noble and honoured spouse of your Amy.

SIR HUGH (*in a milder tone*).

I must, then, give way to your follies, my daughter.

AMY.

You will not regret it, my father. A last word. In the conversation I am about to have with my husband there may be secrets it would be criminal to betray. Promise, therefore, to so place yourself as to see everything and hear nothing. Do you promise?

SIR HUGH.

On my knightly faith.

[*He enters the gallery.*

SCENE IV.

AMY, *then* VARNEY.

AMY (*alone*).

I am, perhaps, wrong in thus eluding the prohibition of my husband. I shall ask his pardon for it. He will understand that I could not allow my father to suffer any longer.—Ah, it is he! [*Running to the door.*] My Dudley!

FOSTER (*announcing*).

Sir Richard Varney.   [*He retires, enters* VARNEY.

AMY (*surprised*).

You, Master Varney! What does this title mean?

VARNEY.

It is a title her Majesty has been graciously pleased to confer on me to-day.

AMY.

Ah, accept my congratulations. But what brings you here?

VARNEY.

The express order of my master, my lady.

AMY.

I was expecting himself.

VARNEY (*presenting the note*).

He has charged me to hand you this.

AMY (*sadly*).

He will not come!

VARNEY.

Matters of importance — his duties near the Queen —

AMY.

I see that my lord has charged you, sir, with a mission to me. Speak, I listen. Well, why do you hesitate?

VARNEY (*with feigned embarrassment*).

It is because — I do not know — what I shall say may offend you, my lady.

AMY.

Nothing coming from my lord can offend me. Speak, Master Varney.

VARNEY (*aside*).

She will not deign even once to address me as Sir Richard. [*Aloud.*] I am charged, madame, to prepare you for a sad change of fortune.

AMY.

What do you mean?

VARNEY.

You must know, my lady, how inexorable is the will of the august sovereign who wields the sceptre of England.

AMY.

Undoubtedly; and what Englishman does not feel a pride in obeying that glorious Queen who has vowed in presence of all her people to live and die a virgin queen?

VARNEY.

If this double title be the cause of your respect for her Majesty, you must lessen that respect by a full half. The approaching marriage of her Highness is commonly spoken of.

AMY.

Yes, indeed, I now recollect there has been some talk of a Spanish or French prince in this connection. Was not King Philip mentioned? or the Duke of Anjou? or was it not rather the Duke of Alençon?

VARNEY.

You are not correctly informed, my lady. The Queen, who might choose a consort from any of the proudest royal houses in Europe, has deigned to cast her eyes on one of her own subjects.

AMY.

Really! The Duke of Lincoln, perhaps?

VARNEY.

He is a Catholic!

AMY.

Perhaps the Duke of Limerick, then?

VARNEY.

An Irishman!

AMY.

In that case the only one left is the Duke of Rutland.

VARNEY.

He is married, — not that that would be much of an obstacle, either.

AMY.

What is this you have dared to say, sirrah?

VARNEY.

A sad truth, madame, if we look to the requirements of State policy. Crowned heads are not subject to the common law, and marriages that trouble thrones are easily broken.

AMY.

How say you, sir? The throne is but the throne, while marriage is the altar.

VARNEY.

Oh, yes! But then, the altar too —

AMY.

Besides, how doth the marriage of the Queen concern me?

VARNEY.

More than you wot of, my lady. Moreover, my Lord of Rutland is not the bridegroom of whom there is question. Among all our English lords, it is not he who wears the coronet of a duke to whom such grace is likely to be done; it is a simple earl.

AMY.

Good God! what do these threatening words conceal? You announce to me a change of fortune. The Queen is at Kenilworth. My husband gives festivals in her honour. Might it be himself?

VARNEY.

It might be himself, madame.

AMY.

Just Heaven! Dudley, my high-souled, generous Dudley deceive and forsake me! He, a peer of England! Thou liest, false varlet!

VARNEY.

I have said nothing, madame.

AMY.

No, but thou hast let me understand everything. To whom art thou traitor here?

VARNEY.

I said well that my words would offend you, my lady Ah, this is far too painful. I retire.

AMY (*arresting him*).

No, remain! I would know—

VARNEY.

I have already said too much. My master did not authorize me to reveal everything; quite the contrary!

AMY.

What! What did he wish you to hide? Speak, I bid you!

VARNEY.

Well, then — the Queen — loves the Earl.

AMY (*prostrated*).

She loves him! And he?

VARNEY.

He, madame? How can it be helped? England desires this marriage. France supports it, the rabble carol it in their ballads, the astrologers read it in the heavens, the courtiers in the eyes of the Queen, and the Queen —

AMY.

And the Queen — finish! — in the eyes of Leicester.

VARNEY.

I did not speak of my lord.

AMY.

But I speak of him! What does my lord think, what does he do?

VARNEY.

What does he think? Only God knows that. What does he do? He hardly knows himself yet. Still, the love of a queen, and of a queen who can make him a king! the need of ever climbing when one has one's foot on the ladder of ambition! of losing all or winning all, — the throne or the abyss! And then to reject a couch which a royal canopy surmounts!

AMY.

I understand!

[*She falls overwhelmed into a chair.*

Marriages that trouble thrones are easily broken, you said? Ah, Leicester, why this profanation? What doth it profit thee to offend God by a divorce and men by a perjury? Dost thou then think I could live after I had lost thy love? Go to! go to! Let sorrow have her way. Thy ambition shall not have long to wait for its freedom!

VARNEY (*aside*).

It begins to work!

AMY (*rising, seized with a sudden thought*).

Ah, but I think only of myself, — and my father? I think only of my love, — and my honour? Once I believed a time would come when I could fling myself on my father's bosom, a proud and happy daughter, loved and respected by her husband. I shall go back to him abandoned like a mistress, dismissed like a servant, without having been for one day, for one hour, acknowledged as a lawful wife.

[*Hiding her head in her hands.*

O the shame of it!

VARNEY (*with feigned timidity*).

If I might venture a word, my lady, I think I could point a means by which you might cease to be Countess of Leicester without ceasing to be a lawful wife.

AMY (*looking at him in astonishment*).

How? I do not understand you, sir.

VARNEY.

If, at the very time when the Earl of Leicester, hurried on by the irresistible bent of his ambition, abandons a treasure grander than all the royalties of the earth, a man were to present himself before you, — a man less brilliant but more trustworthy, — who offered you, instead of a title, illustrious indeed, but which you wear only at the price of secrecy and misconstruction, an honourable name, an alliance proudly proclaimed in the face of the world; if this man —

AMY (*interrupting, and restraining herself*).

Pardon me! You are, if I mistake not, speaking of yourself, Master Varney?

VARNEY.

Well, madame, I am; and I venture to lay at your feet, instead of the selfish and fickle heart you are losing, a deep and devoted love, — a love that would value a single glance of your eyes higher than the smiles of all the queens of earth.

AMY.

And so you offer to make me Dame Varney?

VARNEY.

No, Lady Varney; for such is the title the wife of Sir Richard Varney shall bear, who is no longer an equerry of the Earl of Leicester, but a free knight of the realm of England.

AMY.

But surely you cannot think I may change my name and condition in such easy and simple fashion?

VARNEY.

On the contrary, I do. In the eyes of many, even in those of your father, I am reputed the fortunate person to whom you have given your heart. Permit me, while anxiously awaiting the hour that crowns my happiness, to beg of you to let appearances outstrip reality for the nonce. Her Majesty to-day holds a reception. Let me present you to her as my lawful wife. Accept under —

AMY (*breaking forth*).

Enough! Thou hast unmasked thyself, Richard Varney! So it was to this thy wiles tended, forsooth! Thou wouldst represent Leicester as a traitor to make me one! Thank God! I have seen the snare in time. The desertion with which thou hast threatened me is a lie! This marriage with the Queen, a calumny! Oh, what happiness! Pardon me, my Dudley, for having listened for a moment to this foul-mouthed lackey!

VARNEY.

So you do not believe in the note written and signed by the hand of my lord?

AMY.

I believe that thy treason is twofold, and that thou deceivest us both.

VARNEY.

"All that Varney does, he does by my order and by my will," writes the Earl. It is his will that for his safety and yours I present you to the Queen as my wife.

AMY.

Silence, impostor!

VARNEY.

And beware! His further commands are that if you do not obey, means more violent and terrible —

AMY.

Be still, thou varlet!

VARNEY.

Ah, this is too much! You do not fear, then, to turn my love into hatred? [*Advancing toward her.*] You forget that we are alone, and that you are in my power.

AMY (*alarmed*).

Help! help! my father!

VARNEY (*laughing*).

Your father? Ah, do you imagine that your voice can reach from Kenilworth to Templeton?

AMY.

Father! father! help!

SIR HUGH (*appearing*).

I am here.

VARNEY (*thunderstruck*).

Sir Hugh Robsart!

SCENE V.

The same. SIR HUGH ROBSART.

SIR HUGH.

I am here to answer your call, my child. But, in good truth, there was no need of such precaution and mystery to show me the man who is your husband.

AMY.

You are strangely mistaken, father. This man is not my husband.

SIR HUGH.

He is not your husband! God's blood! Would he refuse —

VARNEY (*quickly*).

Ah, sir, 't would be my greatest happiness and honour to make your daughter my wife. The difficulty does not rest with me.

SIR HUGH.

What? Doth it rest with you, Amy? You must —

AMY.

Father, one single word —

SIR HUGH.

Interrupt not thy father! Bootless to say, I would have preferred for the ancient house of Robsart an alliance with one of older lineage. But Sir Richard Varney is now a knight, and may look for higher advancement, seeing that his master, the all-powerful Earl of Leicester, may be to-morrow the husband of Elizabeth, and King of England.

AMY.

God! What do you say? Leicester? Are you sure?

SIR HUGH.

Did you not know it? I but repeat the universal report.

AMY (*staggering*).

It was true, then! Dudley! O my God!
[*She sinks into a chair.*

SIR HUGH (*running up to her*).

Daughter! She is fainting!

VARNEY (*calling*).

Foster! Janet! [JANET *enters hurriedly.*] Look, your mistress is ill.

JANET (*running to* AMY).

My lady! [*She holds a flask to her nostrils.*

VARNEY (*to* SIR HUGH).

Allow her to come to herself, sir. Her mind, you see, is disturbed. Your presence moves and agitates her.

SIR HUGH.

Yet to leave her thus!

VARNEY.

You shall return, my revered father, when she is in a better condition to listen to you.

SIR HUGH (*looking tenderly at* AMY).

Poor child! Well, I leave.

VARNEY.

Permit me to accompany you. [*Aside.*] And now to find Alasco.

[SIR HUGH *and* VARNEY *go out together.*

SCENE VI.

AMY, JANET.

JANET.

My lady!—my dear mistress! Ah, she opens her eyes.

AMY (*looking earnestly round her*).

My father! Where is he?

JANET.

He will return. You feel better, do you not?

AMY.

Yes, child, yes; I am well. But leave me for a time, Janet, leave me. I need to be alone. Yet stay.
[*Drawing off her bracelets and necklace.*
Take these jewels with you. They weigh me down now!

JANET (*after replacing the jewels in the casket*).

My lady need only call, I shall not be far.

AMY (*alone. She remains motionless for some time and without speaking. She gazes round her with haggard eyes*).

Am I, then, in a dream? Is what Varney said possible? Is it really true? The crime of Dudley is confirmed by the voice of my father! Alas! I am now of such little account in this world, my place therein is so little regarded that men speak before me of that which tortures my soul as an indifferent, or even pleasant, bit of gossip! And so, to-morrow, perhaps to-morrow, there will be no longer, even though death be not one of the guests at Kenilworth, an Earl and Countess of Leicester! He — will be King of England. And I —
[JANET *enters with a silver goblet on a silver-gilt salver.*

JANET.

Madame! — my lady!

AMY (*turning round abruptly*).

What is wanted! Leave me!
[*She recognizes* JANET *and continues gently*
It is thou, Janet! Ah! pardon me —

JANET.

Madame, you are too good to be so unhappy.

AMY.

Yes, very unhappy, dear child! But what dost thou bring me there?

JANET

A soothing potion Foster has bid me take you; it is a composing draught which must needs give you a little rest after all your sufferings.

AMY.

Rest, Janet! There is none for me now, except in the tomb. But put it on the table, and go.

JANET.

Will you drink, my lady?

AMY.

Yes, I will drink. Go, go, my child.

JANET (*aside*).

How pale she is, for a countess!
[*She places the salver on the table near* AMY *and leaves.*

SCENE VII.

AMY, *then* FLIBBERTIGIBBET.

AMY (*alone*).

Innocent, simple people, who believe that the wounds of the soul can be cured by the medicaments of the body! that despair is but a disease, and sleep can be restored to eyes that can no longer weep! Little service can this potion do me, in good sooth! Yet my faithful servants have said to themselves when preparing it: "It will do good to our poor mistress!" Shall I, then, slight their affection? There are but these two hearts in the whole world that feel any love for me, — but this poor maiden and my warder, Foster, who feel compassion for the Countess of Leicester! Since they, at least, have my interest at heart, I owe them the return of showing myself grateful for their cares. I will drink.

[*She takes the goblet and raises it to her lips.*

A VOICE (*apparently from the interior of the wall*).

Do not drink!

AMY (*stopping*).

Who speaks to me?

[*The door of* ALASCO *opens and gives entrance to* FLIBBERTIGIBBET, *who with a bound places himself in front of the Countess.*

FLIBBERTIGIBBET.

I, noble lady. Do not drink.

AMY (*astonished*).

You! Who are you?

FLIBBERTIGIBBET.

Do you not recognize the poor imp whose life you saved?

AMY.

Ah, it is you! But were you not in prison?

FLIBBERTIGIBBET.

Yes, in Mervyn's Tower, behind bolts and bars, in a frightful dungeon, which you reach by a parlous gallery, the floor of which sounds terribly hollow.

AMY.

You have been able to escape, then?

FLIBBERTIGIBBET.

Despite my nimbleness as a goblin, I don't think I could have wrought such a miracle as that. No, I was released by an older devil, whose earthly name is Alasco. There is a secret passage running through the wall which leads from my cell to his laboratory. Oh, don't imagine it was the kindness of this worthy Alasco that prompted him to free me! He did so on certain conditions. One was that I should undertake the delicate task of putting you to sleep. And the nature of the sleep? I am ignorant of it. I could only catch the gist of a few words during a rapid dialogue between your Varney and my Alasco. Varney had come in search of a draught ordered by the Earl of Leicester, and intended for the Countess. 'T was all I could learn.

AMY.

But what is the nature of this draught?

FLIBBERTIGIBBET.

There can be no mistake about that.- It comes from the kitchen of Alasco. It must be poison.

AMY.

Poison! and is it Leicester that sends it?

FLIBBERTIGIBBET.

Yes; he gave the order to have that draught composed for you.

AMY.

Pardon me, O my God!
[*She again takes the goblet and raises it quickly to her lips.*

FLIBBERTIGIBBET (*arresting her arm*).

What are you doing, madame? It is poison, I tell you! Did you not hear me?

AMY.

Yes, I have heard you; but since Leicester sends this poison, I must drink it.
[*She raises the goblet anew to her lips.* FLIBBERTIGIBBET *snatches it from her.*

FLIBBERTIGIBBET.

No! you once saved my life, and it is my turn now! To hell with this devil's broth!
[*He dashes the goblet on the ground.*
You shall see this floor grow as black before an hour, as if Beelzebub himself had breathed on it.

AMY (*gazing fixedly on the spilt liquid*).

What have you done, and what is going to become of me, now that I have no more poison?

FLIBBERTIGIBBET.

Become of you, noble lady? By the genius of Shakespeare! between a husband who seeks to divorce you by poison and a Varney who is hankering after you, there is but one course by immemorial usage in all tragedies, comedies, and pantomimes, — flight!

AMY.

Why should I fly, and where?

FLIBBERTIGIBBET.

Eh! Have you no family? — a brother, or a father?

AMY.

My father! Yes, you are right, my father! Ah, surely now I am released from my oath! I will tell all to my father! I shall at least die justified and pardoned. Yes, let us fly! But how?

FLIBBERTIGIBBET.

By this window, which is hardly a story above the trees of the park. Yesterday I wanted to frighten Alasco, through the window, and did so by means of a ladder, which I afterwards hid in the thicket. [*Leaning out of the window*]. It is there still. You can easily descend with my help. It is mere child's play, madame!

AMY.

I consent. Make haste, then; I am in a hurry to meet my father!

FLIBBERTIGIBBET.

Wait! Are you forgetting nothing?
[*He takes the cloak lying on the back of the chair.*
This cloak. [*Looking at the table.*] What is this parchment? A pass from the Queen! Heavenly powers! We must not leave behind us this precious viaticum!
[*He hides the parchment in his bosom.*
Now, come, come, madame!

AMY.

May God watch over us!
[FLIBBERTIGIBBET *aids her in stepping from the casement.*

ACT IV.

SCENE.—*Kenilworth Park. At the back, in the distance, the roofs of the new castle are seen through the trees. On the right, the Fountain of Neptune.*

SCENE I.

AMY; FLIBBERTIGIBBET, *entering abruptly.*

FLIBBERTIGIBBET.

Your flight has been discovered, madame. Alasco and Foster are searching for you in the woods. Fortunately, one is old and the other dull-witted, and this bushy, rolling corner of the park is wonderfully well-adapted for a game of hide-and-seek.

AMY.

But I must have some information; I must know where to find my father.

FLIBBERTIGIBBET.

If I could leave you alone an instant, I would soon bring Sir Hugh Robsart to you. But take care! There are people coming in this direction! Good heavens! 't is the Earl of Leicester with his worthy equerry!

AMY (*bitterly*).

Leicester and Varney! the two conspirators!

FLIBBERTIGIBBET.

Come, madame, come! All is lost if they see us!
[*He hurries her into the coppice on the right.*

SCENE II.

Leicester, Varney.

LEICESTER.

Speak quick! The Queen has nearly finished her walk along the lake. I am in a hurry to join her.

VARNEY (*violently excited*).

My lord, you were a witness that I was able to make the Queen understand that my wife was very sick and in no fit condition to be presented to her Majesty. Well, I have just learned that the Countess has fled! It is worse than resistance, my lord, it is rebellion.

LEICESTER (*thoughtful*).

I cannot impute this resistance as a crime to her, Varney; or, if it were a crime, it was a crime of love.

VARNEY.

But, my lord, the Countess exposes you to the danger of being charged with falsehood —

LEICESTER.

She has ever walked in the path of honour and loyalty. That path must be mine too, Varney, and not the one you would have me tread.

VARNEY.

The road in which you are leads to greatness, to supreme power.

LEICESTER.

Yes, by falsehood and treason.

VARNEY.

Ah, my lord, it is now too late to retreat. Elizabeth, blinded by her own passion rather than by you, has shown a want of self-restraint that, while it permits you to hope everything, ought to make you fear everything. The day on which she opens her eyes, the awaking will be terrible. Bethink you what the fury of an outraged woman can do when that woman is a queen. Take care! It is not your lands and honours merely that are at stake, it is your life! And the safety of the Countess is worth as little as yours. The Queen might spare the man whom she loves; would she spare the rival whom she abhors?

LEICESTER.

It is just this danger to Amy that makes me pause. I must, at all cost, defend and save her.

VARNEY.

And how? A subject cannot struggle with his Queen.

LEICESTER (*reflecting*).

No, and I will not make the attempt. But to-morrow, perhaps, the Queen will be no longer at Kenilworth. Then —

VARNEY (*in terror*).

Great God! my lord, you are not thinking of leaving England! You will not, good my lord, by exile fling to the winds the most brilliant fortune that man has ever dreamed of!

LEICESTER.

A fortune with which yours is closely bound, is it not, Master Varney? However, I reckon on your devotion —

VARNEY.

My lord!

LEICESTER.

Well, well, let the Countess be sought for,—not to take her away from here, but that I may have discourse with her. Let us now go to the Queen. [*He goes out.*

VARNEY (*following him, aside*).

If he leave the country I am a ruined man! If he see the Countess I am a dead man! [*He joins* LEICESTER.

SCENE III.

FLIBBERTIGIBBET, AMY, *then* VARNEY.

FLIBBERTIGIBBET (*coming out of the thicket and following* LEICESTER *and* VARNEY *with his eyes*).

They are going away. You can come out safely from your fortress of briar. But take care of your beautiful eyes, for never have I seen branches more disposed to caress them than those, with their thorns too. [AMY *appears.*]

AMY.

To think that I am actually hiding from Leicester as from an enemy!

FLIBBERTIGIBBET.

And I go now to seek your natural protector against this enemy,—your father. Do you keep quiet in the angle of that fountain. Should necessity require, you can easily reach the coppice from it.
[*He conducts her to the fountain.* VARNEY *appears at the back.*

VARNEY (*aside*).

I really think I saw Flibbertigibbet. [*Seeing* AMY.] Ah. the Countess! What would it be wise to do?

What if I dared? 'Twould be a very bold stroke! But audacity has helped me so far, and I am in such extreme peril that I must risk all to save all. [*He retires.*

FLIBBERTIGIBBET (*to* AMY).

Wait for me here, my lady. Before a quarter of an hour I shall return with Sir Hugh. [*He goes out.*

AMY (*alone*).

I deserted my father for my husband, and now I have but one single idea, — to leave my husband for my father. Leicester, is it possible that after trying to pass me off as the wife of thy lackey, thou hast wished to poison me? Alas! he who can commit a base act can also commit a crime! Where now is the great Earl, the noble Dudley? All is over between us. There is not in my soul one spark of love for him; it has been extinguished by my scorn. I do not even hate him.

[*She sits down, pale and motionless, on the shaft of a column, near the fountain. The Queen appears.*

SCENE IV.

ELIZABETH, AMY.

ELIZABETH (*reading a note*).

What means this mysterious summons? "Let the Queen come alone to the Fountain of Neptune." Well, I am here. [*Discovering* AMY.] Who is this woman?

AMY.

The Queen! O heaven! the Queen, it is the Queen!

ELIZABETH.

What is that? Woman, what art thou doing here?

AMY.

Your Majesty — I was passing by. I beg leave to withdraw —

ELIZABETH.

No, speak. Thou dost seem disturbed and almost fainting. Take courage, girl, thou art in presence of thy Queen.

AMY.

Madame, 't is why I tremble.

ELIZABETH.

Take courage, I say! Hast thou any grace to beg of us?

AMY.

Madame — I beg your protection, madame.
                [*She falls on her knees before the Queen.*

ELIZABETH.

Each daughter of our realm hath right thereto while she is worthy of it. Stand up and come to thy right mind. Why, and in what, dost thou crave our protection?

AMY.

Madame — I cannot tell! Alas! I know not.

ELIZABETH.

Why, this is mere folly, girl. We are not accustomed to ask questions so oft without receiving an answer!

AMY.

I entreat, — I implore your Majesty, — let me be restored to my father.

ELIZABETH.

But I must first know this father of thine. Who art thou? Who is he?

AMY.

I am Amy, daughter to Sir Hugh Robsart.

ELIZABETH.

Robsart! In good sooth, I have, for two days, been much busied anent the affairs of this family. The girl asks me for her father, the father asks me for his daughter. Thou dost not yet say all that thou art. Art married?

AMY.

Married! O God! then you know all, madame? Yes, it is true! Forgive me! forgive me in the name of Heaven, most gracious lady!

ELIZABETH.

Forgive thee, girl? Eh! for what should I forgive thee? That is the concern of the father thou hast deceived. Thou seest I know all thy story; thy blush avouches it for true. Thou hast let thyself be seduced, carried off —

AMY (*proudly*).

Yes, madame; but the man who seduced and carried me off was my husband.

ELIZABETH.

In truth, I know thou hast repaired thy fault by marrying thy ravisher, — the equerry Varney.

AMY.

Varney! Oh, no, madame, no! As there is a heaven above me, I am not the degraded wretch you would make me! I am not the wife of that contemptible villain Varney!

ELIZABETH.

What! what does this mean? Methinks, wench, thou canst talk fast enough when the subject liketh thee! [*As if to herself.*] Of whom am I the dupe here? There is some shameful mystery or other under this. [*Aloud.*] Amy Robsart, it was in the presence of the noble Earl of Leicester, his master, that Varney declared himself thy husband —

AMY (*sadly*).

In presence of the Earl —

ELIZABETH.

Yes. But tell me, woman, whom hast thou married? Tell me — for by God's light I will know — whose wife or whose paramour art thou? Come, speak out, and be speedy! for thou wert better dally with a lioness than palter with Elizabeth of England.

AMY.

Ask the Earl of Leicester; he knows the truth.

ELIZABETH.

Leicester! The Earl of Leicester! Woman, thou dost belie him! Who has set thee on to this odious falsehood? Who has suborned thee to slander the noblest lord and truest-hearted gentleman of our realm? Come with me instantly. — But here he is himself in search of us. [*Raising her voice.*] This way! this way! Were he closer to us than our right hand, thou shalt be confronted with him, thou shalt be heard in his presence that I may know if there be in all England any man so distraught as to lie to the face of Harry VIII.'s daughter!

SCENE V.

AMY, ELIZABETH, LEICESTER, VARNEY, *all the Court.* ELIZABETH, *her eyes fixed on* LEICESTER; AMY, *pale and fainting.*

LEICESTER (*aside with a terrified gesture*).
O Heaven! Amy, with the Queen!

ELIZABETH (*aside*).
How pale he looks! [*Aloud.*] My Lord of Leicester, knowest thou this woman?

LEICESTER (*in a low voice*).
Madame —

ELIZABETH (*violently*).
Knowest thou this woman, my Lord of Leicester?

LEICESTER.
Your Majesty will permit me to explain —

ELIZABETH.
Hast thou dared to practise a deception on me, — on me, thy benefactress, thy confiding and too partial sovereign? Thy present confusion doth seem to avouch thy treason. If 't is so, by all that is holy, false Earl, thy perfidy shall meet its due reward!

LEICESTER (*dejected*).
I have never wished to deceive you, madame.

ELIZABETH.
Silence, my lord! That head of thine standeth in as great peril as ever did thy father s!

AMY (*aside*).

O God! —

LEICESTER (*drawing himself up proudly and speaking in a firm voice*).

My head, my sovereign liege, cannot fall but by the sentence of my peers. At the imperial bar of the parliament of England will I plead my cause, and not to a princess who thus requites my faithful service. The sceptre of your Majesty is not a fairy's wand to build a scaffold in a day.

ELIZABETH.

What! My lords, you have heard! We are defied, I think, braved in the very castle we have bestowed on this proud man! My Lord of Shrewsbury, you are Earl Marshal of England. Attach him of high treason.

AMY (*aside*).

O my God! I thought I no longer loved him!

ELIZABETH.

Raise not thy head so haughtily, Earl of Leicester. Our father of glorious memory hath ever caused those heads to fall that listed not to bend. Good cousin of Hunsdon, order out your band of gentlemen pensioners, and take the traitor into instant custody. Take from him his sword, and be speedy about it. We have spoken.
[HUNSDON *draws his sword; three gentlemen advance toward* LEICESTER, *who stands calm and motionless.*

AMY (*running and throwing herself at the feet of the Queen*).

No, no, madame! Pardon! justice! He is not guilty! he is not guilty! No man can accuse in aught the noble Earl of Leicester!

ELIZABETH.

Well, in good sooth, wench, this is a marvel! Didst thou, thyself, not accuse him an instant ago? Hast thou, then, belied him?

AMY.

Did I accuse him, madame? Ah! if I did, then, of a truth have I belied him, and I alone deserve your anger.

ELIZABETH.

Beware, insensate woman that thou art! Didst not thou, thyself, say, a moment ago, that I had but to question thee to discover that the Earl of Leicester was privy to thy whole history?

AMY.

I did not know what I was saying, madame; they practised on my life, I was mistaken, my reason was upset —

ELIZABETH.

Who then is thy husband, or thy paramour, Amy Robsart, if as thou hast just now affirmed thou art not the wife of Varney?

LEICESTER (*advancing*).

I must confess to your Majesty —

ELIZABETH.

My lord, let the woman speak.

AMY.

Madame! [*Aside.*] O heaven! [*Aloud.*] Yes, madame, I am the wife of Varney!

LEICESTER (*aside*).

My self-devoted Amy! Ah, if in endangering myself I did not endanger her as well!

ELIZABETH.

And so thou dost confess, young woman, that all the disorder of which thou art witness has been caused by thine impudent lies and silly imposture? Dost thou admit thou camest hither with intent to slander the illustrious Earl of Leicester, and ruin him in our esteem?

AMY.

It seems I must admit it.

LEICESTER (*aside*).

Ah, her devotion rends my heart. [*Aloud.*] Beseech your Majesty, deign to hear me —

ELIZABETH (*smiling*).

In an instant, dear my lord, pray you. Let us have the pleasure of seeing your innocence established without your aid. Your enemies have suborned this wretched creature. Allow us to question her.

VARNEY (*advancing*).

Gracious lady, she is not as guilty as seemeth to your Majesty. I had hoped her misfortune might have remained concealed. But the Queen must have perceived that her reason hath lost its balance, and —

LEICESTER (*aside*).

Wretch!

AMY (*aside*).

It behooves me to endure the sacrifice to the bitter end.

ELIZABETH.

By my troth, Sir Richard Varney, I rather lean to the belief that thy master's enemies have used thy wife as a tool wherewith to weaken his standing in our regard, though they have but strengthened it withal. Let this woman be led to the prison of the tower, until we take further thought as to her disposal. Lord Hunsdon, to you I commit the prisoner. Have her strictly watched, and give orders that no one — not even the lord of this castle — have approach to her, unless he have a safe-conduct signed by our own hand. You hear, my lord.

[LORD HUNSDON *bows and takes away* AMY.

LEICESTER (*aside*).

O misery! mine own beloved Amy!

AMY.

At least, if I die now, 't will be for him!

ACT V.

SCENE.— *Interior of the round tower of the dungeons. Old Norman architecture. A cone-shaped roof. In centre of back an iron door; to the right of this door, a small grated window. On the left a couch. An immense piece of timber, serving as a support for the base of the roof, crosses the tower in the upper part.*

SCENE I.

AMY *alone, seated on the couch, pale, her hair in disorder.*

AMY.

The sacrifice is finished! I do not know how it is I have become almost a State criminal, seeing that my only faults have sprung from my love. The Queen is my rival! the Queen! and her anger will not touch me except to some dread purpose. To-day the prison; to-morrow — Dudley, they told me thou didst wish to take my life. I will anticipate that wish of thine and give it to thee freely. For thee the throne, for me the grave. I shall vanish, and thou remain with this Elizabeth who is a queen O dismal thought! when she thrills in his embrace I shall be lying stretched on my lonely and icy couch in the tomb! O agony! How bitter and harrowing is jealousy to one about to die!

[*She hides her head in her hands and weeps. At this moment a door on the right in the wall, hidden by some carved work, opens; it turns noiselessly on its hinges, allowing* FLIBBERTIGIBBET *to enter, and then closes of itself in the same manner.* FLIBBERTIGIBBET *advances slowly a few steps, and then stands in front of* AMY, *who has not lifted her eyes.*

SCENE II.

Amy, Flibbertigibbet.

AMY (*without seeing* FLIBBERTIGIBBET).

And is not this dungeon itself death? Am I not out of reach of the living world? Where is the ear that could hear my voice? Where is the hand that could touch mine?

FLIBBERTIGIBBET (*without changing his posture*).
Here.

AMY.

Who is there?

FLIBBERTIGIBBET.

Flibbertigibbet, at your service.

AMY.

You! Are you, then, in very truth, a sorcerer or a goblin that you have been able to enter this impenetrable prison, and that too, may Heaven pardon you for it, without a door being open?

FLIBBERTIGIBBET.

Unfortunately, God has nothing to forgive me in this matter, noble lady.

AMY.

But how have you entered?

FLIBBERTIGIBBET.

By the way which you shall leave by.

AMY.

I cannot understand —

FLIBBERTIGIBBET.

It is very simple.

[*He points to the concealed door.*

There is a door there.

AMY.

Indeed? Where does it lead to?

FLIBBERTIGIBBET.

I have already told you. It leads by a secret stair to the laboratory of Alasco, and from thence to the chamber whence you have escaped once, and whence, with the help of God or the devil, you shall escape a second time. But make haste! By some lucky chance or other, Alasco has gone out. He may return at any moment, and then escape would be difficult. Come, madame, come.

[*He takes a step toward the secret door.*

AMY.

I thank thee, my poor friend, but I cannot follow thee.

FLIBBERTIGIBBET.

What?

AMY.

Hie thee away at once! If thou wert discovered here —

FLIBBERTIGIBBET.

Yes, I am so anxious about myself! But you?

AMY.

I remain.

FLIBBERTIGIBBET (*stamping*).

Oh, now, this is too bad! Do you think I have come here for the purpose of going away as I came? Do you think I am going to leave you here in this cold, damp atmosphere with the owls and bats, with cobwebs about your bed and jailers at your door, while outside the air is

pure and free, and plain, forest and river delight the eye?
If you wished me to let you die in this cell, why did
you save my life?

AMY.

I cannot help it, my friend. Am I not condemned
to death by him to whom my life and soul belong?
Though I were at liberty, what could I do with my freedom? Is not Dudley unfaithful to me? Has not
Dudley desired to poison me? Has not Dudley abandoned me to his Varney? Is not Dudley about to wed
Elizabeth?

FLIBBERTIGIBBET.

Tush, tush! that is an old story, madame. The scene
has changed. Your Dudley is not unfaithful, he has
not attempted to poison you, he never thought of giving
you up to his equerry, Devil-Varney, and, far from
intending to wed the Queen, he is, at this moment, plotting an act of high treason, — namely, your rescue.

AMY (*clasping her hands*).

Could this be possible? Are you telling the truth?

FLIBBERTIGIBBET.

It was Varney alone who planned everything, who, in
fact, concocted the whole plot.

AMY.

Ah, it is, then, as I thought at first! O my Dudley,
how much I have wronged thee!

FLIBBERTIGIBBET.

That is not all; your father knows of the marriage,
and has been reconciled to your husband. Both are now
adopting means to save you; they are, perhaps, both
waiting for you outside. Will you still stay here?
Will you keep them waiting?

AMY.

Oh, no! quick! quick! Lead me at once to my lord! lead me to my father!

FLIBBERTIGIBBET.

Good! The bolt is drawn! Let us lose not a second! Follow me!

[*He runs to the concealed door and tries to open it; it resists. He makes a fresh attempt; it is useless. The door neither moves nor opens. He turns in consternation to* AMY *who has been looking on, trembling.*

FLIBBERTIGIBBET.

Shut! The door is shut and bolted on the outside! Alasco and Varney have returned. That room which they left vacant was a snare.

AMY.

And so you are lost on account of your attempt to save me. Hapless wretch that I am, my misfortune is contagious.

FLIBBERTIGIBBET.

Beseech your ladyship, do not speak of me! I have nothing to lose. It is you who lose everything!

AMY.

Yes, I am again plunged back into the night of my dungeon! The last glimmer of hope is quenched.

FLIBBERTIGIBBET (*drawing himself up*).

The last? Not so, dear and noble lady! We must never despair. Your father and husband are at this moment taking measures for your safety. I wonder if I might see them from the window.

[*He brings a wooden stool to the casement, mounts it, and stands on tip-toe in order to see the outside.*

The sun is descending behind the trees of the park. We have but a quarter of an hour of daylight. Ah! what do I see yonder in the shadow of the twilight? Two men muffled in cloaks. They are coming toward the tower. They are stopping at the foot of the wall. They are measuring it with their eyes. Madame, it is they! My lady, it is they!

AMY.

They? Who?

FLIBBERTIGIBBET.

Your father! your husband!

AMY.

My husband! my father! Are you not mistaken? Let me look!

FLIBBERTIGIBBET.

Look, madame.

[*He leaps down from the stool.*]

AMY (*taking his place at the window*).

Ah, my God! It is, it is my husband! my Dudley! Ah, how hard it is to see through these bars! [*Calling.*] Husband! father!

FLIBBERTIGIBBET.

The tower is too high for them to hear you. But shake your handkerchief, they may, perhaps, see it.

[AMY *waves her handkerchief outside the bars.*

AMY.

Yes, yes, they see it; they raise their hats. But [*sadly*] I see them and they cannot see me!

FLIBBERTIGIBBET.

No matter! they are warned and will deliver you.

AMY (*shaking her head*).

Deliver me!

FLIBBERTIGIBBET.

Yes, surely. What doors do not open before the lord of this castle? He has power and he has gold.

AMY.

That will not suffice to-day. He cannot enter the tower. Thou knowest not, my poor friend, what are the orders of the Queen? No one can enter here,—no one.

FLIBBERTIGIBBET.

What! not even the Earl of Leicester, the all-powerful minister?

AMY.

He less than any other. No one enters, I tell you, unless he have a safe-conduct signed by the hand of the Queen.

FLIBBERTIGIBBET.

Good! Then it is a royal pass that is wanted?

AMY.

Undoubtedly.

FLIBBERTIGIBBET (*drawing a parchment from his pocket*).

Here it is, madame.

AMY (*taking the parchment*).

What! the Queen's signature! Now, once for all, this must be magic!

FLIBBERTIGIBBET.

Hardly even foresight. I fouhd this talisman yesterday on your table.

AMY.

Ah, yes, I remember! My father's pass.

FLIBBERTIGIBBET.

I have done well not to forget it, as he did. Quick now, madame; wave your handkerchief again, and throw the parchment to your rescuers.

AMY (*waving her handkerchief*).

They have seen the signal.

[*She throws the parchment.*

May God guide it safely to its destination!

FLIBBERTIGIBBET.

Follow its course with your eyes. What is happening to it?

AMY.

It is falling. It whirls about. It is now above the trees.

FLIBBERTIGIBBET.

Pray God it do not nest in one of them!

AMY.

No, it is still falling. Ah, it is now on the ground before them.

FLIBBERTIGIBBET.

Have they seen it?

AMY.

They have!

FLIBBERTIGIBBET.

We are saved!

AMY.

My Dudley is kissing the parchment. He is making me a sign. They are both making for the postern. The angle of the wall hides them from me. I no longer see them.

FLIBBERTIGIBBET.

But you shall see them soon again, and very near, noble lady.

AMY (*descending from the window*).

Blessed be God!   [*She looks at her disordered garb.*
He will soon arrive. In what a condition I am to receive him! My gown quite rumpled, my hair in disorder —

FLIBBERTIGIBBET.

A good sign, that! Sorrow is giving way to vanity! But I think I hear something or other walking.
  [*He listens at the iron door.*
It is the tread of men. How is it that the floor of that corridor sounds so hollow?
  [*The sound of a key turning in the lock is heard.*
They are opening it, madame, they are opening it!
[*The door at the back opens. Enter* SIR HUGH *and* LEICESTER.

SCENE III.

The same. LEICESTER, SIR HUGH.

AMY (*rushing into the arms of* LEICESTER).

My lord!

LEICESTER (*pressing her to his heart*).

My beloved!

FLIBBERTIGIBBET.

A moment ago she was as pale as a corpse, and now she is as rosy as a bride! These young women change colour oftener and faster than the Star of Aldebaran.

LEICESTER.

You must be wroth with me, Amy. How shall I ever expiate the wrongs I have done you? Say that you forgive me!

AMY (*still hanging on his arm*).

Ah, it is thy part to forgive, noble Earl! Why did I dare to suspect thee? [*Turning to* SIR HUGH.] And you too, my father, have you forgiven me? Do you forgive?

SIR HUGH (*holding both her hands clasped in his*).

My child! My daughter!

FLIBBERTIGIBBET.

Meanwhile, as the door is open, why do we delay?

LEICESTER.

He is right. Time is precious. Listen, darling; everything is prepared for my escape and thine. In an hour a carriage shall be waiting for us in the wood. Trusted friends, among them Strathallan, the Earl of Fife, will protect our flight. A brig, ready to sail for Flanders, will receive us on the coast; and before daylight dawns, we shall be sailing together, free, wafted to happiness by favouring breezes, — thou far from thy prison, I far from the Court!

AMY.

What! my lord, dost thou, for my sake, abandon rank and honours, power and fortune, and that brilliant theatre on which thou wert the admired of all Europe? What sacrifices you make for a poor woman!

LEICESTER.

This poor woman, as you call her, has made many for me.

AMY.

You condemn yourself to exile!

LEICESTER.

Art thou not my country?

AMY.

Dudley, thou renouncest everything.

LEICESTER.

Nay, rather nothing, since thou art everything for Dudley.

AMY.

Who knows? Perhaps even a throne?

LEICESTER.

A throne? Go to! By leaving the Queen to follow thee, I renounce, something tells me, the chance of climbing, not the steps of a throne, but the ladder of a scaffold!

SIR HUGH.

My lord, forget not that while you speak, this imperious Queen is waiting for you.

LEICESTER.

Yes, we must leave thee awhile, dear wife!

AMY.

Why so? Do you not lead me with you?

LEICESTER:

Not yet. In an hour the Queen quits Kenilworth. At this moment her retinue fills every part of the castle, and thy escape would be impossible. I go to hold her stirrup, and when she leaves I shall return here. Kenilworth will then be deserted, and by favour of the friendly night, I shall carry thee off from this hideous dungeon.

AMY.

It will be the second time you have carried me off, my lord. Ah, forgive me, father!

LEICESTER (*to* FLIBBERTIGIBBET).

Do thou, lad, follow us. I shall have need of thy service in arranging matters when I am in attendance on the Queen.

FLIBBERTIGIBBET.

I am at your orders, my lord.

AMY.

Am I, then, to be again alone?

LEICESTER.

For an hour, at most, my beloved!

AMY (*hanging on his neck*).

Dost thou remember, my lord, it was by the sound of thy horn thou didst give warning of thy presence in the woods of Devon in the early days of our love? Well, to please me, wilt thou announce thy return this evening in the same fashion?

LEICESTER.

I promise thee to do so; meanwhile, be happy and without fear. Farewell.

AMY.

Farewell.

[*They embrace. The Earl goes out with* SIR HUGH *and* FLIBBERTIGIBBET.

SCENE IV.

AMY (*alone*).

Farewell! — There is something ominous in that word; it is as if they who uttered it bade each other meet in eternity and not till then.

[*She sits on the couch and muses.*

They are now far away; I no longer hear their footsteps. I am once more alone. I know not why it is, but sad thoughts come trooping to assail me. Am I not about to be happy? Nay, am I not happy now? Am I not about to be free, — free to see him, to hear him, free to love him? Oh! mind and body are both sick unto death; the emotions of this day have crushed all my energy. Would it not be well to snatch a few moments' rest before beginning this journey which is to lead me to happiness?

[*Gradually her voice grows weaker and her body seems to be weighed down.*

O my Dudley, what a sweet future is ours! Exile, 't is true; but exile with thee! — some secluded, obscure abode; long days spent near thee, at thy side; a life all freedom and love, — provided that this be not a dream!

[*She falls asleep.*

SCENE V.

VARNEY, ALASCO.

At the moment when AMY *falls asleep, the concealed door half opens.* VARNEY *passes his head through the opening, as if assuring himself that all is safe. After concluding that the Countess is asleep, he enters, lead-*

ing ALASCO *by the hand who appears to follow him with reluctance and impatience.*

VARNEY.

She is asleep. [*To* ALASCO.] Quick! come, I say! come!

ALASCO (*placing a lighted copper lamp on a stool*).

What do you mean by dragging me after you in this fashion? My time is not so worthless that I can afford to waste it in listening at doors in your company. I was busy at a critical moment on my great work. I had three retorts on the furnace, filled with such a perilous substance that were the least drop of it to fall into the fire, this tower would be shattered to pieces.

VARNEY.

Alasco, hast thou heard?

ALASCO.

I was not listening.

VARNEY.

The Earl of Leicester is going to fly, — fly with his wife! and if he succeed in his purpose, in a few hours the favourite will be an exile, and the favourite's equerry shall fall from the point he reached, a hundred times lower than the point from which he started!

ALASCO.

What is that to me!

VARNEY.

What is it to you? The goods of the outlaw will be confiscated, and the domain of Cumnor with the rest. Then, good-bye to thy laboratory, thy alembics, thy pharmacy of philters, thy cookshop of poisons! Now, dost see what it is to you?

ALASCO.

Well, what is the cause of all these mishaps? The escape of this bird. Go, inform Elizabeth of it, and the cage will not open.

VARNEY.

Yes, but it will though! It will open to receive the Earl. Elizabeth will send Leicester to consummate his marriage with Amy on the scaffold. And what shall Varney gain by that?

ALASCO.

The thanks of the Queen for having undeceived her.

VARNEY.

The thanks of the Queen? Say her hatred, rather! I shall inspire her with horror. And even if my good offices escaped punishment, the best I could hope for would be to be forgotten.

ALASCO.

You need not tell her it was Leicester that planned the escape of his wife.

VARNEY.

Then he continues to be the all-powerful favourite, and sooner or later, his vengeance is sure to reach me.

ALASCO.

But then, if every course is bad —

VARNEY (*coming close to* ALASCO).

Not every one! Alasco, if fate laid a heavy hand on this woman, this wretched Amy, who has caused the Earl to do so many foolish things; if she disappeared from the world; if she died — a natural death — how dost thou think it would affect Leicester?

ALASCO.

He would forget her. He would continue the successful minister, the omnipotent favourite, the great Earl who gives festivals and entertainments to the Queen.

VARNEY.

And we too, Alasco, we too would continue our peaceful progress in his train, advancing as he advanced, and finding ourselves earls or barons on the day when he would awaken king.

ALASCO.

Yes, just as you say, — Baron Varney, Prince Demetrius Alasco!

VARNEY.

So there is but one obstacle between us and fortune, — it is the life of this woman.

ALASCO.

And what do you intend doing with the obstacle?

VARNEY.

Remove it!

ALASCO (*with a gesture of terror*).

Oh! I thought you loved this woman?

VARNEY.

She has called me lackey! I hate her. [*Half drawing his dagger.*] To think that an inch of steel in that proud heart would sweep away the impediment that checks the career of so many brilliant destinies!

[*He makes a step towards* AMY.

ALASCO.

Varney! Varney! a stab! 'T will be known as thine!

VARNEY.

Thou 'rt right. Well, hast thou not — hast thou not some elixir, some poison, to even breathe which is death?

ALASCO.

A poisoning! 't will be known as mine!

VARNEY.

Then what is to be done?

ALASCO.

Whatever thou listest. This business likes me not. I care not to meddle with it. A woman! — and a woman in her sleep!

VARNEY.

Thou art a coward!

ALASCO.

And besides, as I told thee already, my crucibles are waiting for me.

VARNEY.

Thou art a madman! [*He appears to be musing for some moments.*] What is to be done? What is to be done? — Ha! a natural death? A death that leaves no trace behind it? [*Striking his forehead.*] By heaven! I have it. Is not this tower the tower of the dungeons? Alasco, the floor of the narrow corridor that leads from this cell has a trap-door outside the very threshold of the door.

ALASCO.

Well!

VARNEY.

Touch a spring and the supports which sustain the trap fall, which, thereupon, keeps its position level with the floor by a slight adhesion, and yet is undistinguished from it. The slightest pressure on this trap would suffice to hurl her into the abyss beneath.

ALASCO.

Well?

VARNEY.

Now, the Earl has left the door open. Wait for me a moment.

ALASCO.

Where art thou going?

VARNEY.

To press the spring that drops the supports of the trap.

[*He goes out by the door which has remained open, and which half closes in such a way as to hide the corridor.*

ALASCO.

What foul plot is this hell-hound hatching? And my elixirs that are burning away yonder! — Well, Varney!

VARNEY (*returning*).

It is done! Now woe to whoever sets foot on that trap! A touch as light as a sylph's would launch the luckless intruder into eternity!

ALASCO.

Surely thou wilt not seize the prisoner and hurl her into that gulf?

VARNEY (*with a sneering laugh*).

Oh, fie! what brutal fancies thou hast! I will not touch the prisoner.

ALASCO.

Then I don't understand.

VARNEY (*lowering his voice*).

Didst thou not hear the Earl promise to warn his wife of his return by the sound of the horn?

ALASCO.

Well, what follows?

VARNEY.

Follows? Dost thou think that when the captive hears that sound she will have patience to wait until her lord comes here? Dost thou think she will pause an instant before running to meet him? Well, if in her thoughtlessness she pass this door, if the worm-eaten props of the trap give way beneath her, if she fall, how can I help it? Will it be my fault? It will be an unfortunate accident simply.

ALASCO.

To destroy her by means of her best affections! It is a seething of the kid in the mother's milk!

VARNEY.

And now let us retire. The Earl cannot be long now. Return, if thou list, to thy damned crucibles. I will remain on the watch behind the concealed door.

[*They both go out.*

SCENE VI.

AMY (*alone*).

Deep silence reigns in the cell, which is only lit by the copper lamp on the stool, forgotten by ALASCO. *After a few moments' silence and sleep the sound of a horn is heard outside.* AMY *awakes with a start.*

AMY.

What noise was that that woke me? Was it not the sound of my lord's horn? [*She listens.*] Nothing but the wind whistling through the crannies of the wall. 'T was what, perhaps, aroused me. So much the better! I have had a fearful dream.

[*The sound of a horn is again heard.*]

Yes, I was not mistaken; it is the horn, it is the signal. [*She runs to the casement.*] Torches, horses, armed men. Yes, it is my Dudley! He alights from his horse, he is helping my father to alight. How handsome he is, my Dudley! Ah, that door is open! I will hie me to meet him, and so spare him the trouble of returning to this prison.

[*She wraps her veil about her and kneels.*]

O God, to thy care do I commend myself!

[*The horn resounds for the third time.*]

Dudley, I am thine!

[*She takes the lamp, pushes the door open and disappears. When the door falls back to its place a shriek is heard, and a crash like the fall of heavy beams of timber. Then the small door opens and* VARNEY *appears, pale and shuddering.*]

SCENE VII.

VARNEY *alone. He enters slowly, with haggard eyes.*

VARNEY.

Is it done? Ay, I heard the crash. No one here. It is done. Well, all is over! Beshrew thee, Varney, art thou afraid? [*With a horrible chuckle.*] The lamb hath fallen into the pit of the wolf, is that a cause for trembling? If I were to see —

[*Advances to the door, then starts back and returns.*
To see? What boots me seeing? I have heard. It is enough. Rejoice, Richard Varney, from this hour dates thy fortune!
[*Suddenly a great noise is heard behind the concealed door. It opens violently. A red, flickering glimmer is seen, and* ALASCO, *deadly pale, rushes with a cry of horror on the stage.*

SCENE VIII.

VARNEY, ALASCO.

ALASCO.

Ah, woe to us, Varney!

VARNEY.

Alasco! What aileth thee, pray?

ALASCO.

Ill betide us! A curse is on our works!

VARNEY.

What?

ALASCO.

Varney, my alembic hath exploded, the tower is half fallen and the castle on fire!

VARNEY.

What sayest thou, thou wretch? The castle on fire?

ALASCO.

Look!
[*The glare gradually grows stronger. The flames are heard hissing outside.*

VARNEY.

Great God!

ALASCO.

We have no time to lose. The conflagration is travelling fast. Let us fly!

VARNEY.

Yes, let us fly!

[*They run to the iron door.* ALASCO *pushes it and recoils appalled before the open gulf on the threshold.*

ALASCO.

Devil! what abyss is this?

VARNEY.

It is the trap of the dungeons.

ALASCO.

A gulf impossible to cross! Flight or safety is impossible. On one side, this chasm; on the other, fire! Death! death! there is only death!

VARNEY.

'T is thy fault, poisoner!

ALASCO.

'T is thine, assassin!

VARNEY (*pointing to the blaze*).

Who caused that fire?

ALASCO (*showing the open trap*).

Who opened yon gulf?

[*The conflagration makes* **rapid** *progress, the flames come through the concealed door, the roof splits, the wall cracks, sparks fall thick as hail from the pinnacle of* *the tower. At this moment* FLIBBERTIGIBBET *passes through a breach in the roof and appears standing on the transversal beam of timber beneath.*

SCENE IX.

VARNEY, ALASCO, FLIBBERTIGIBBET.

FLIBBERTIGIBBET.

Varney! Alasco!

VARNEY.

Who calls? Is it hell?

FLIBBERTIGIBBET.

Hell is content to wait for you. Reproach not one another! 'Tis I who have caused the explosion of the alembic. 'Tis I who punish ye.

VARNEY.

Ah, thou accursed imp of the devil!

FLIBBERTIGIBBET.

Fiends who murdered an angel! Follow ye her into yonder gulf. Ye shall not follow her farther!

[*He disappears through the opening in the roof, which sinks, and buries* VARNEY *and* ALASCO *beneath it.*

THE END.

www.ingramcontent.com/pod-product-compliance
Lightning Source LLC
LaVergne TN
LVHW031630070426
835507LV00024B/3409